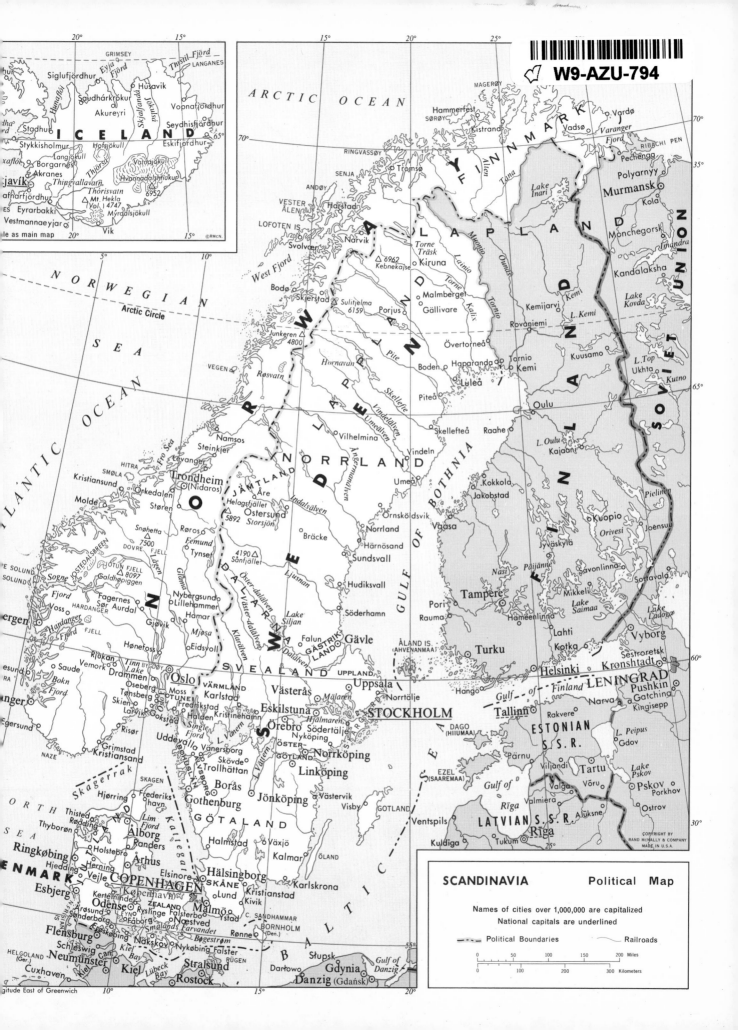

LIFE WORLD LIBRARY

SCANDINAVIA

TIME
LIFE
BOOKS
®

LIFE WORLD LIBRARY

SCANDINAVIA

by Hammond Innes
and The Editors of LIFE

TIME INCORPORATED   NEW YORK

COVER: Fishing ships mantled
with crisp snow lie in the iced-over waters
of a small but busy harbor
in the Lofoten Islands, rocky arctic outposts
of the Norwegian fishing industry.

ABOUT THE WRITER

Hammond Innes, author of the interpretive text for this volume in the LIFE World Library, is a distinguished British writer whose novels are characterized by a wealth of factual reporting and well-authenticated backgrounds. A onetime journalist who has traveled widely in Scandinavia, Mr. Innes in 1960 published *Harvest of Journeys,* a nonfiction chronicle of the many expeditions he has made in search of material for his novels. He returned to Scandinavia in 1962 to complete his research for this book. Perhaps the best known of the many international bestsellers he has written is *The Wreck of the Mary Deare,* a 1956 novel set in the English Channel, which he has sailed for years in his own boats. Also flavored by the sea he loves are his more recent novels, *Atlantic Fury* and *The Strode Venturer.*

Contents

TIME-LIFE BOOKS

EDITOR
Maitland A. Edey

TEXT DIRECTOR   ART DIRECTOR
Jerry Korn   Sheldon Cotler

CHIEF OF RESEARCH
Beatrice T. Dobie

Assistant Text Director: Harold C. Field
Assistant Chiefs of Research:
Monica O. Horne, Martha Turner

•

PUBLISHER
Rhett Austell

General Manager: Joseph C. Hazen Jr.
Circulation Director: Joan D. Manley
Marketing Director: Carter Smith
Business Manager: John D. McSweeney
Publishing Board: Nicholas Benton, Louis Bronzo,
James Wendell Forbes

LIFE MAGAZINE

EDITOR: Edward K. Thompson
MANAGING EDITOR: George P. Hunt
PUBLISHER: Jerome S. Hardy

LIFE WORLD LIBRARY

SERIES EDITOR: Oliver E. Allen
Editorial Staff for *Scandinavia:*
Assistant Editor: Jay Brennan
Designer: Ben Schultz
Staff Writer: David S. Thomson
Chief Researcher: Grace Brynolson
Researchers: Paula von Haimberger Arno, Mary Elizabeth Davidson,
Irene Ertugrul, June Omura Goldberg, Nancy Jones,
Helen R. Turvey, Linda Wolfe

EDITORIAL PRODUCTION
Color Director: Robert L. Young
Copy Staff: Marian Gordon Goldman, Carol Henderson,
Dolores A. Littles
Picture Bureau: Margaret K. Goldsmith, Joan Lynch
Art Assistants: James D. Smith, William Gedney

Valuable assistance in the preparation of this book was given by the following individuals and departments of Time Inc.: Larry Burrows, Howard Sochurek, Nina Leen and Carl Mydans, LIFE staff photographers; Mark Kauffman and Marvin E. Newman, Time Inc. contributing photographers; Knud Meister, Copenhagen correspondent; Doris O'Neil, Chief of the LIFE Picture Library; Richard M. Clurman, Chief of the TIME-LIFE News Service; and Peter Draz, Chief of the Bureau of Editorial Reference.

Introduction

In recent years our attention has been so often fixed on crises in Berlin or the Congo or South Vietnam that the countries of Scandinavia have not received the attentive recognition commensurate with their remarkable accomplishments. These peaceful, strong, prosperous nations offer great beauty and a persuasive good sense. It is worthwhile, therefore, that Hammond Innes and the Editors of LIFE have given us a book that contains generous quantities of both.

The Scandinavian countries are no longer among the great powers of the world, but their economic strength, their sense of international responsibility, their efficiency and their adherence to the ideals of democratic society give them an influence—a deserved influence—far beyond their size.

The three northern bastions of the free world —Norway, Sweden and Denmark—own more than 10 per cent of the world's shipping and command almost 5 per cent of international trade. Yet they have less than 1 per cent of the world's people. But from these few have come giants in the arts and sciences, and giants, too, in the quest for peace and international cooperation. For who would care to guess what would have become of the United Nations had there been no Trygve Lie and no Dag Hammarskjöld?

There is so much in Scandinavia to appreciate, enjoy and even copy; the prose of Mr. Innes and the pictorial essays which accompany it make this volume an excellent introduction to all three kingdoms.

W. WALTON BUTTERWORTH
former U.S. Ambassador to Sweden

The great Sogne Fjord, calm and deep, winds inland from the sea past tall peaks, small villages and tiny neatly cultivated fields. It is

still a much-used waterway, as it was in the days of the Vikings.

1

Kingdoms of the North

A LAND of fjords and the midnight sun—
that is the image of Scandinavia created
by the travel agencies. It is no myth. The
fjords of the Norwegian coast are one of the
scenic wonders of the world, great glacier-
scored gashes up which the largest liners can
sail; the Sogne Fjord, the most spectacular of
all, cuts 112 miles into the mountains, its towering rock walls rising to 5,000-foot heights
near the great white expanse of Jostedalsbreen,
continental Europe's largest glacier. Above the
Arctic Circle the lighthouses are almost unnec-
essary during the summer months; this is a
world where the sun does not set and people
sleep with their blinds drawn against the unending summer day. It is a fairy-tale world
composed of sea and rock and forest, where
the mountains are capped by eternal snows
and great glaciers push their icy snouts to the
edge of sheer precipices, where Lapps drive
huge herds of reindeer, and seabirds crowd the
nesting ledges. The dominant factor in the

shaping of these northern lands was the ice of successive glacial periods which scoured the surface rock, deposited loads of silt and in retreat relieved the land of its staggering weight and allowed it to rise. The result is a deeply indented coast littered with islands.

But this is only a part of Scandinavia. Farther south, the land is less austere. The warm beaches are thronged with sun worshipers, and the rolling, fertile plains dotted with sturdy, brightly decorated farmhouses. Reminders of an earlier era—carefully preserved older sections of towns, dramatic castles, graceful manor houses—stand in pleasing contrast to modern, balcony-festooned apartment buildings, well-laid-out factories and the clean lines of functional schools.

WHAT is Scandinavia? There are a number of definitions. Geographically, it is simply the great mountainous peninsula which droops for 1,200 miles like a curved nose from the northernmost reaches of Europe, and which includes only Norway and Sweden. In common usage, Scandinavia encompasses three kingdoms—Denmark, Norway and Sweden. Scandinavia is also sometimes said to include Iceland and Finland, but in recent decades the term *Norden*—the North—has been more generally applied to these five countries as a group. The sparsely populated island of Iceland was originally colonized by Norwegian Vikings and soon fell under the control of first Norway, then Denmark. It did not regain its independence until World War II. Finland was an integral part of Sweden for more than 650 years; today, although most of its people speak Finnish, which is unrelated to any major European language, almost 10 per cent of the population still learn Swedish as their mother tongue.

In 1809, during the Napoleonic Wars, Sweden was forced to cede Finland to Russia. The country did not secure full independence until World War I, when the Russians were involved with the internal struggles out of which arose the Soviet state. In the winter of 1939-1940, when the Russians invaded it, Finland fought desperately and successfully to maintain its independence, but it was forced to cede territory to the Russians. Hoping to regain the land, Finland advanced into Russia in 1941 after the Soviets had reopened hostilities. After the war, it was forced to surrender additional territory, to pay enormous reparations and to enter into a mutual-defense pact with the Soviet Union. Today, Finland maintains a watchful independence in the shadow of its massive neighbor.

Although their country has strong links with its western neighbors, the Finns have always seemed to some degree a people apart, and they have often expressed a feeling of separateness and individuality. "How young, how youthful is this people!" wrote the Finnish philosopher Eino Kaila in 1959, expressing the "hope that [their] future will include an ever-deepening contact with Scandinavia."

For all the ties with Finland and Iceland, the heartland of Scandinavia comprises the three kingdoms—Denmark, Norway and Sweden—and it is these countries to which this volume gives primary attention. They were briefly united under one crown in the 15th and 16th Centuries. Their languages have a common root. Their peoples have not very much difficulty understanding each other. In internal political thought they are all of one mind—socialist democracies, with monarchs shorn of real power.

SINCE World War II the tendency has been for the three kingdoms to become even more closely linked. Passports for travel between them have been abolished, as have work permits. Thus a common labor market has been created. A Swede, for example, may take a job in Norway without formalities. In addition, Norway gives him the same social-welfare benefits, like health and old-age insurance, that it grants its own nationals, even though he may remain indefinitely in Norway. A Norwegian traveling in the opposite direction enjoys similar privileges.

A major instrument in these and similar cooperative moves has been the Nordic Council, a group formed in 1952 of representatives from the parliaments and governments of the three countries and of Iceland. Iceland, however, does not participate in the common labor market nor in the exchange of all social-welfare benefits. Finland became a member of the Council in 1956, after the Soviet Union had relaxed its bitter criticism of the organization. Although Finland takes a full part in council activities, its representatives are carefully enjoined by their government from participating in any possible discussion of "questions relating to military policy or which might result in commitments in conflicts of interests between Great Powers."

Despite their many links, the Norwegians, the Swedes and the Danes remain distinct and individual peoples with their own very recognizable characteristics. One of their common denominators is the sea. And yet it is the sea as much as anything else that is responsible for their individuality.

Norway, alone among the three, has a long oceanic seaboard. For more than 1,000 miles this long ribbon of a country is bordered by the Atlantic. The southernmost tip is at the same latitude as the northern reaches of Labrador, and Nordkapp, in the far north of Norway, is on a level with Baffin Island and the northern coast of Alaska. With the Arctic Circle cutting the country a bare two thirds of the way up the coast, it should be a bitter, frozen land, but the prevailing southwesterlies and an extension of the Gulf Stream, that warm ocean current sweeping up from the Gulf of Mexico, combine to give it a mild climate and keep the ice at bay. Some 150,000 islands and massive rocks guard the coast from the full fury of Atlantic gales so that for hundreds of miles the Inner

THE THREE KINGDOMS working together are symbolized in the insigne of the Scandinavian Airlines System, which shows the similar flags of the monarchies: red and white for Denmark *(top, left)*, red, white, blue for Norway *(top, right)* and blue and yellow for Sweden. SAS is a part-private-, part-government-owned company operated jointly by the three countries.

Lead provides safe natural communications. Man began infiltrating this coast some 10,000 years ago, moving in from the south and east as the ice receded. Forest and fish—there was nothing else to provide him with the bare essentials of existence.

The mountains and the sea have stamped the Norwegian with their character. Life is hard and man himself is hardy, self-reliant; rocklike and possessed of that wonderful kindliness and dependability that is the birthright of all men who live by the sea.

These children of the midnight sun seem a part of the open air. Norwegians combine hard work with a physical, outdoor existence that probably has no counterpart in Europe; the mountains to hike through, a ski slope behind almost every village, and the sea, always the sea, with summer homes on the islands and a large proportion of the population in possession of a boat of some sort. And it is not only the country people who have this love of the open air; the people of the cities and the industrial workers have it, too, using their cars or bicycles as a means of transporting themselves to the countryside. In fact, the working day itself, beginning early and often finishing about four in the afternoon, is organized to meet this fetish for the open; the *middag*, or main meal, is eaten immediately after work to give a long, uninterrupted evening. And because they are people of the open air, the Norwegians have an almost frontier-post quality of friendliness, allied with a natural shyness and informality.

In the far south of Scandinavia—in Denmark —there is another west-facing coast, that of Jutland. It is far less important than Norway's fjord-sliced western seaboard, for it is a dune coast with few ports. Treacherous tides gave it a wicked reputation in the days of sail. Its people, too, are rugged; tough like the west coast Norwegians, they traditionally earn their livelihoods by fishing the North Sea banks, launching their boats into the sea from the spray-lashed dunes.

Between these two very dissimilar western coasts is the strait of the Skagerrak, which leads into the Kattegat and thence through the Sound or through the Little or Great Belts to the inland Baltic Sea. These are just the major waterways; there are unnumbered others. In the south, low-lying Denmark is parted by shallow ribbons of water that still go by the name of fjords. The largest of these, the Lim Fjord, zigzags across the north of Jutland. A boat can sail into it by the fishing port of Thyborøn on the west coast and, following 100 miles of dredged channels, come out into the Kattegat. Indeed, so indented is Denmark by the sea's inlets that it has a coastline of 4,600 miles—longer than that of the seaboard of the United States from California to Washington. Little wonder then that its people are seafarers by nature. Once they were among the formidable sea powers; they remain great traders and shipbuilders.

There is a marked difference in temperament among the Danes. East of the Jutland dune coast, where the land becomes more fertile, the country richly agricultural, the people are softer, more easygoing. More than a quarter of the population lives in and around Copenhagen. A glance at the map helps to explain why this is so, for the most direct route into the Baltic

is through the narrows of the Sound, and Copenhagen commands the narrows. It is thus one of the principal transit ports in northern Europe, and trading and manufacturing installations have grown up around it.

Copenhagen is in a way the most sophisticated of the three Scandinavian capitals. Architecturally it is enchanting—a sky line of copper spires, green against the wide expanse of the sky. Here the Baltic countries make their contact with the wider world beyond the seas and oceans. The atmosphere is gay. People at the executive level are less reserved, easier to talk to, and their linguistic range is greater than in the other two Scandinavian countries. People on the street, too, are often proficient in English and other languages. Leading journalists, besides reading several of the top British and American newspapers and magazines, regularly will sift through the German, French, Belgian and Italian press; they may even have a working knowledge of Russian. In addition, of course, they read the publications of the other Nordic countries. The Danes' interest in the world is perhaps a heritage of past centuries when Denmark, as the geographical bridge between central Europe and the more northerly countries of Scandinavia, served as the conveyer of European cultural influences. The Danes take great pride in their cosmopolitanism. But though they have a very broad knowledge of world trends, they seem less decisive than other Scandinavians, perhaps for that very reason.

Norway's capital of Oslo, some 300 miles north of Copenhagen, is smaller, more parochial. Its location helps to make it so, for it

---

SOME PRONUNCIATION HINTS

The Scandinavian languages share a number of characteristics. In all of them the letter "j" is pronounced like "y" in English and "w" is like "v." The letter "ø" in Norwegian and Danish, as well as the letter "ö" in Swedish, is pronounced the same as the "u" in "turn." In Norwegian and Swedish the "skj" and "sj" are both heard as "sh" (Hammarskjöld is hammershuld). The "å" in all three (which is sometimes written as "aa" in Norwegian and in Danish) has a sound similar to the "o" in "ford" (Årøsund is awrasun and Haakon is hawk-un). The "ae" in Danish is usually pronounced like the "a" in "able," but "ae" in Norwegian is like "a" in "cat." The "ä" in Swedish is pronounced like the "e" in "end" (Älvsborg is pronounced elves-bor).

lies at the head of a 60-mile-long fjord. Although it has one of the most beautiful approaches of any city in the world, Oslo is not architecturally exciting the way Copenhagen is. Nevertheless, it does have something of the same atmosphere, for the Norwegians, like the Danes, are a happy people. American visitors may well envy them their apparently carefree existence. There are times—and the midpoint of the 20th Century is one of them—when small countries appear to have advantages over large and powerful nations with worldwide commitments and responsibilities.

It must be remembered, however, that small nations are faced with disadvantages, too. In World War II both Denmark and Norway were overrun by the Germans. Throughout history their geographical position has made them vulnerable to the shifts of European power politics, and today the Soviet Union looms very large when viewed from the western end of Russia's primary exit to the Atlantic. Both the Danes and the Norwegians are very conscious of their vulnerability, economically as well as politically. Nevertheless, the sense of happiness and contentment is striking.

BETWEEN the Danes and the Norwegians on the one hand and the Swedes on the other there is something of a gulf. Although all three are linked by trade, culture and political cooperation, the visitor to Scandinavia soon becomes conscious of the disparity. It is fundamentally one of temperament. Sweden's population is larger, the country richer. Sweden has earned its wealth by the greater drive and efficiency of its people, although it is in fact blessed with greater resources than the other two. The Swedes are industrialists as well as traders, and the country has produced a harder, apparently colder people. The mood is expressed by the architecture of their capital, Stockholm. It is solid, almost overpowering. The mood is expressed, too, in the greater formality of social life. In general, the Swedes seem a much less relaxed people than the Danes and the Norwegians.

This Scandinavian gulf, although one of temperament, has been to some extent aggravated by political pressures. The shock felt by the West at Russia's belligerent behavior at the end of World War II is almost forgotten now, so accustomed has the world become to the cold war, but in 1948 it came as a deadly political chill to Scandinavia. That was the year that the Communists took over Czechoslovakia, Finland came under pressure and the Berlin blockade reached its height.

The question then for all three Scandinavian countries was how best to preserve their independence in the face of the new line-up of powers. Norway was still attempting to rebuild after the debacle of World War II, as was Denmark. Moreover, flat little Denmark had no illusions about its ability to withstand attack. It never has had any since the humiliation of its defeat in war with Prussia and Austria in 1864, when the victors took possession of Schleswig-Holstein. In 1948 well-armed Sweden offered the other two Scandinavian countries a neutral defense pact. In 1939 such an alliance, backed by sufficient arms, might have proved an effective discouragement to the Germans, but now the opposing camps appeared to have grown too large, the world too small. Neither Denmark nor Norway believed that even the combined power of Scandinavia would be sufficient to protect them from the Russian threat. They dickered about the proposal, but both finally allied themselves to NATO and the West, and Sweden was left in solitary Nordic isolation.

SWEDEN'S geographical location inevitably delimits its freedom of action in international affairs. The great central spine of the Scandinavian mountain ridge cuts it off from Norway and the Atlantic. Its other land frontier is with Finland in the north. This is a short border, but with no natural obstacles. Moreover, Finland at that point is less than 200 miles across. Beyond Finland is Russia. Sweden's eastern sea frontier then sweeps 750 miles southward. Across the narrow Gulf of Bothnia and the Baltic, the country faces the southern regions of Finland;

the old Baltic states which are now incorporated in Soviet Russia; and Poland and the East German republic, both of them satellites of the Soviet Union.

This proximity to Soviet power has caused the Swedish people, committed as they are to western democratic institutions and philosophies, much heart-searching and much expenditure of wealth and effort for armaments. The Swedes have no wish to arouse Soviet hostility by abandoning their neutral posture, and they fear that a formal alignment with the West might bring the Soviet Union to apply more overt pressures on neighboring Finland and, conceivably, on their own borders.

While Sweden today is indisputably a western-oriented nation, its original thrust was eastward. It was in that direction that the bulk of its men moved in the great period of Viking expansion. Its relics of that era are consequently of less personal interest to the western world than are the relics of Norway and Denmark, whose Vikings, in the main, took their ships on westward expeditions.

It is only within the last century that much of the evidence of the Norsemen's voyages has come to light—the Tune, Oseberg and Gokstad vessels preserved virtually intact near Tønsberg and Sandefjord in Norway, the ship grave at Ladby on the island of Fyn in Denmark, and others on the European mainland. In these cases, the Viking's ship and personal equipment had been included in the burial mounds, to the present benefit of boat enthusiasts and all students of this early mercantile period when the men of the north sailed west to America and south to the coasts of Africa.

UNFORTUNATELY, none of these countries is rich in buildings of the Viking period. Towns and villages were constructed of the material most ready to hand. The ice age left a land clothed in fir and spruce, and because the soft wood of these trees was more easily worked than the native rock most of the old structures were built of timber. Little remains, for the resinous wood was highly susceptible to fire. The Norwegians, in particular, have been at great pains to establish open-air folk museums where the visitor can wander from farmhouse to stave church and see relics brought from all parts of the country for preservation there with loving care.

BECAUSE of the physical nature of these northern countries the early settlements were largely isolated. Mountain, forest, glacier, river, fjord and sea—these kept communities apart. As a result the social structure was based on the separate entities of individual settlements. The physical circumstances that bred the Norsemen, while encouraging military and political organization, inevitably slowed the process of cultural development.

Something of this parochialism remains to this day—in western and northern Norway, for example. There is less of it in Denmark and Sweden, both countries more susceptible to continental influences. It must be remembered that in the mountainous north of Norway it was only a short time ago that the expansion of industry provided the inducement necessary for the construction of roads, which are extremely difficult and expensive to build there. Previous communication was mainly by sea. The construction of bridges to replace the innumerable ferries as a means of communication between the main islands or across fjords is also a recent development.

In considering Scandinavia, therefore, it is necessary constantly to bear in mind the obstacles nature has placed in the way of intercommunity contact, particularly the great mountain wall running north and south, dividing Sweden from Norway; to bear in mind also that these countries have all had one natural, God-given means of communication in common—the sea. Scandinavians are by necessity—and therefore by tradition—a maritime people. The sea is in their blood. So, too, are the physical features of the North—the mountains and the forests, the lakes, the fjords. It is against this background that the peoples of Scandinavia must be assessed.

Office girls ascend an escalator at the central Hötorget station of Stockholm's subway, which is adorned with chewing gum posters.

Rapidly Shifting Currents of Change

Few if any of the cities of Europe are as thoroughly urbanized as the large centers in Scandinavia. Housing developments, tall buildings, shopping centers and traffic jams increase daily. City planners work to reorganize communal patterns. The sky line changes and with it many of the habits and attitudes of the people. Yet outside the cities, away from the machines, the rhythms of nature are still strong and a rugged, almost primitive way of life goes on.

OLD RITUALS still
mark the turning year
and keep alive
the fervor and magic
of centuries past

TRADITIONAL FETE of St. Lucia's Day
begins with a procession led by a girl
wearing a candle-studded crown *(left)*.
Observed since medieval times, this
saint's day (December 13) officially
starts the Swedish Christmas season.

MIRACLE PLAY draws large crowds
each summer *(opposite)* to Leksand
on Sweden's Siljan Lake, where folk
dramas and dances are popular. The
play, a Christian allegory, is given
in a natural outdoor amphitheater.

DARING STILTWALKER impresses the girls as he navigates on sunny steps in the old section of Bergen. The Gulf Stream helps make Norway's short summers warm.

ARDENT SUN BATHERS in brief bikinis *(right)* try to tan as much skin as possible during a summer vacation at Tylösand, a popular beach resort on Sweden's coast.

SUN-SEEKING CROWD listens to band music at a large and excellent outdoor restaurant *(below)* at Skansen, a fine park on one of the islands in Stockholm's harbor.

joy to young and old as they rush outdoors to make the most of its brief yearly visit

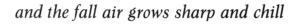

ROUGH BOATHOUSES protect small fishing craft when the foul weather arrives. Norway's fjords are so numerous that they make the actual coastline some 12,400 miles long.

A LONELY FARM nestles by a fjord *(left)* in the shadow of steep mountain walls. Some Norwegian farms are virtual cliff dwellings perched on ledges high above the water.

DEEP WINTER locks the land in an icy embrace for long months of bleak days
.

SNOW-COVERED RACKS hung with drying codfish dot the island towns of northern Norway, where the men fish throughout the dark winter. Although some of the natives paint their houses in gay colors, this remains a dun land of rocky shores, fish warehouses, severe white churches and long, hard toil in sub-zero temperatures.

LARGE CITIES grow larger as country people flock to share in their pleasures

NEW SUBURB of Stockholm called Farsta *(above)* forms a small city in itself with housing, parks, industry and shops. Farsta is one of several carefully planned new suburbs built to relieve congestion in Stockholm proper.

HEAVY TRAFFIC pulses through central Stockholm *(opposite)* toward the tall new Wenner-Gren Administrative Center for scientific research *(background)*. A growing net of subways will ease the chronic traffic problem.

SIDEWALK CAFE with crisp lights, neat chairs and scrubbed brick terracing *(right)* draws smartly dressed Stockholm urbanites. Highly cosmopolitan, Stockholm borrows customs and fashions from other European cities.

STUDENTS chat between classes in a park near the University of Oslo campus. Norwegian youths, unlike their more blasé Swedish counterparts, still crave adventure.

CITY YOUTH, benefiting
from postwar prosperity,
seek new fads to help them charm
the hours of an ample leisure

TWISTERS at a Stockholm amusement park take a rest (above) as others (below) do an energetic version of the dance. Styles in dress and dance show American influence.

COUPLES sway to the persuasive swing of America's Count Basie at an open-sided dancing pavilion in Göteborg, Sweden, the girls wearing their coats against the evening chill. Along with girls and jazz, Swedish boys love automobiles, and joy riding in "borrowed" cars has become a considerable police problem in recent years.

In an old print, a Viking ship sails up an inlet on the coast of Greenland, which Erik the Red settled around 986. Some 15 years

later his son, Leif Eriksson, explored the North American coast.

2

The Viking Age

ALTHOUGH they are referred to as "hosts" and "hordes," and have been likened to a swarm of locusts, their numbers were not great. They were, however, a tough, virile and very lusty people. They raided and traded in most of the then known world and explored far beyond its reaches. They were the Vikings, the Norsemen, the men who poured out of the northlands, and so formidable was their impact that they gave their name to an era. To this day, the period from the Eighth midway through the 11th Century is referred to by historians as "the Viking Age."

There is a great deal of academic argument about the origin of the term Viking. That it stems from the Old Norse word *vik*, meaning a creek or inlet, seems too simple an explanation for the experts. Some suggest that it derives from *vig*, meaning battle. This seems a possibility, for the Vikings loved combat. Indeed, the Viking who died in battle was assured of being carried by the Valkyries, the swift maidens who chose the dead, to Valhalla, the Norse heaven in which dead heroes roistered forever with the gods. Others believe that it comes from *Viken,* meaning men from the Oslo region known as the Vik; still others that it derives from the Latin word *vicus,* a district or settlement. Some scholars produce the verb *vikja,* meaning to deviate; the noun derived from this, *viking,* would then mean one who makes a journey from home.

The best-known monuments to the Viking Age lie preserved at Bygdøy, a section of Oslo. Here, in the Hall of the Viking Ships, lie the Tune, Gokstad and Oseberg ships found in burial mounds between the years 1867 and 1904. The building with its steep-pitched roofs has a stark austerity, the dead white of the interior setting off to perfection the blackened wood of vessels that were interred in the protective blue clay and peat at the end of the Ninth and beginning of the 10th Century. Few visitors to Norway's capital fail to make the pilgrimage to Bygdøy, and many of those who stand and wonder at the delicate beauty of these ships are descendants of people who had every reason to dread the Viking.

BUT these are not ships of the frightful hosts. They are not long ships. In fact, their beam is considerable and this, with the shallowness of their draft, gives them a delicate skimming-dish look, like elongated, pinched-out saucers. The Oseberg ship, 70 feet long and 17 broad, is shaped more like the *karvi,* or coastal vessel, of the time and was probably a pleasure ship. The Gokstad ship, larger and sturdier, had room for 16 pairs of oars, but it could sail and even beat to windward. A replica of it built in 1893 did, in fact, cross the Atlantic in 28 days, a remarkable performance.

The long ships in which the Vikings ranged over almost the entire known world were even larger and more seaworthy than these. They were called *dreki,* or dragon ships, and their size was measured by the number of "rooms" —the spaces between deck beams in which the rowers sat. The average warship, according to

Björn Landstrom, the Finnish artist and nautical expert, had 20 rooms and was 100 feet long. The old Viking sagas report that Canute, the Dane who became king of England in the 11th Century, had a 60-room dragon ship, a monstrous vessel with space for 120 oars and a total length of 260 feet.

EVEN allowing for some exaggeration in the case of the Canute boat—the sagas were after all a form of advertising—these are still relatively long ships; five centuries later Columbus' *Santa María* was less than half this length. These big dragon ships represent the ultimate in development of the early hide-and-wood boats pictured in Scandinavian rock carvings, the result of almost 3,000 years of progress in the art of boatbuilding. Their perfection ushered in one of the most savage periods in European history.

At the end of the Eighth Century A.D. the Vikings fell upon the neighboring lowlands, and in the course of the next 200 years and more the dreaded long ships plowed the waterways of the world until the Norsemen had fought their way into territories almost as large and diverse as those that had constituted the Roman Empire.

It was brutal and piratical; the burning, the plundering, the slaughtering—nothing was sacred. Christian culture, based on church and monastery, reeled before the onslaught. The first raid on the British Isles recorded by the Anglo-Saxon Chronicle came in 787 from western Norway. In 793 the Holy Island of Lindisfarne was sacked. The scholar Bede's old monastery at Jarrow in the northeast of England was attacked the following year; thereafter the pirate fleets raided rich, soft Saxon England in ever-growing numbers. From the peats and meres of Jutland the Danes roved westward to the North Sea and Channel coasts. From the northern fjords the Norwegians descended on Scotland and the islands of Orkney, Shetland, Faeroe, the Hebrides and Ireland. All Scandinavia seemed suddenly on the move, an expansionist wave solidly based on the seafaring craft of a people skilled in the arts of battle.

As man upsets the balance of nature at his peril, so kings, disturbing the delicate balance of power between opposing countries, weaken the foundations of their realms. When Charlemagne, following the Frankish conquest of the Frisians, subdued Saxon Germany, he removed the buffer between his Christian empire and the pagan north. At the same time the population of the Scandinavian world was outstripping the ability of the rugged land to support it. Perhaps more important to the men of the northlands was the lure of piracy, plunder and trade. Like locusts they sprouted wings—the wings of oar and sail. They were filled with the soaring spirit of adventure. And they had a sharp, brutal weapon. Centuries of forest-dwelling had led to the perfection of the iron ax for felling trees and constructing dwellings. The ax made possible the building of the long ships. And it was the ax that was to spread terror into the hearts of the Christian world.

THE Vikings had something else, too. The tribal life of their small communities, centered on their inlets, had developed in them a great sense of camaraderie. Isolated and constantly at war with the forces of nature, they understood the advantages of combining. They were trained to what the British in the days of empire called "the team spirit" by the close confines of shipboard life as well as by the rigors of the climate in which they lived. The full extent of this ability to combine for the mutual good was not immediately apparent, for the early depredations were essentially small-scale operations. But as the young jarls, or earls, sailed summer after summer against the northern shores of Britain and across the Baltic Sea to the rich plains of Europe they gained confidence. Probing the weaknesses of Charlemagne's widespread empire, they came to realize how vulnerable were the land-based forces of the Frankish dominions against the mobility of their own ship-borne raiding parties. It was then that the Vikings began to combine their forces, gathering under elected leaders in fleets

so large that they came to be called "the hosts."

But almost a century was to pass before this happened. Meanwhile the Vikings probed farther and farther afield. In 802 they sacked the beautiful island monastery of Iona in the Hebrides. Then from Scotland they moved again on Ireland, destroying a rich monastic culture. Until Charlemagne's death in 814 they attempted little on the continent of Europe and even left southern England in peace. The men of the Norwegian and Danish long ships, circling Britain north and south, met in Ireland to squabble over the spoils. But two decades later, the easy plunder of the coastal monasteries exhausted, the Vikings moved up the rivers of Europe, up the Rhine and the Seine. Paris itself was attacked. They reached Spain, fought with the Moors and stretched their sails to Iceland.

And then in 859 they passed through the Straits of Gibraltar and into the Mediterranean. The greatest period of Viking expansion had dawned, an incredible penetration by a mercantile power of half the world.

The most daring thrust was westward, from Iceland to Greenland and on to the coasts of America. Trouble at home was now the spur. Scandinavia was consolidating, the individual becoming subject to the greater power of kings. For the rebel, the hard-drinking, roistering jarl of the type who spear-pointed the thrust into the Atlantic, colonization and further exploration were the only answers.

FOR knowledge of this continued westward movement, we are dependent on the Icelandic sagas. These give Garda as the first Viking to sight Iceland. He circumnavigated the island in 850. The first settlements were established some 20 years later. By the end of the Ninth Century, there were 25,000 people permanently settled in Iceland, and large numbers of ships were trading back and forth between the island and Scandinavia. These voyages and colonies were probably an important factor in the development of the Norsemen's mercantile and colonizing instincts, which were to have

Reykjavik (874)
Greenland (986)
Vinland (c.1000)
(North American coast)
ICELAND
Faeroe Is. (870)
Shetland Is. (c.800)
Orkney Is. (c.800)
Hebrides (c.800)
Iona (802)
Isle of Man (798)
Lambay (795)
Dublin (834)
Chester (894)
Portland (789)
Nantes (843)
La Coruña (844)
Lisbon (844)
Seville (844)
Cadiz (844)
ATLANTIC OCEAN
NORWAY
SWEDEN
NIDAROS
SKIRINGSSAL
BIRKA
DENMARK
HEDEBY
LANELAW
York (867)
London (850)
Jarrow (794)
FRISIA
Cologne (881)
Quentovic (842)
NORMANDY
Paris (845)
Seine R.
Rhine R.
Garonne R.
Ebro R.
KINGDOM OF ASTURIAS
CALIPHATE OF CORDOVA
Camargue (859)
Balearic Is. (860)
Pisa (860)
BAY OF BISCAY
NORTH SEA
BALTIC SEA
MEDITERRANEAN SEA
Wollin (960)
Staraya Ladoga (800)
Novgorod (820)
Kiev (820)
Dnieper R.
Don R.
Volga R.
Sarkel (c.960)
Itil (914)
Semender (969)
CASPIAN SEA
Danube R.
BLACK SEA
BYZANTINE EMPIRE
Constantinople (860)
CALIPHATE OF BAGHDAD
Baghdad
Tigris R.
Euphrates R.

Areas of extended Viking occupation and settlement
* Main starting points of Viking raids

VIKING RAIDS AND EXPLORATIONS ranged far and wide in the Eighth to 10th Centuries. Most of these expeditions originated in the Scandinavian settlements marked above by stars. Dates on which the Vikings arrived in various locations are given in parentheses. Some of the voyages were plundering raids, particularly in southern England and what is now France. Others—particularly those in eastern Europe and beyond—were for the purpose of setting up trade routes. Sometimes the warriors and traders stayed only a short time. But in the areas indicated by diagonal shading they stayed for protracted periods, in time merging into the native populations.

a very marked effect on the history of Europe.

The sagas say that as early as 900 a longship skipper named Gunnbjörn, blown off course, sighted the towering icecaps of Greenland. But not for another 80 years did the exiled Erik the Red, banished from the Iceland settlements and sailing with 30 others and their cattle, head west for the new land. Undaunted by the ice of the east coast, he rounded Cape Farewell, Greenland's southern tip, and in three years explored most of the ice-free western shores. In 986 he sailed from Iceland again, this time at the head of 25 vessels laden with emigrants and cattle. Fourteen ships reached the promised land, and the 300 people they contained founded the first Greenland colony. Fifteen years later the Greenland settlement was a thousand strong, spread over 300 miles of coast, established within 500 miles of the American shore.

Unfortunately, there is no record of any Greenland sagas. Traces of the settlements of Vestribygd and Eystribygd are to be found in stone and turf houses and the ruins of churches. These are all that remain of the Greenland colonists, for Greenland possessed none of the mildness of the Icelandic climate. Instead of the Gulf Stream, it was the cold Greenland Current that washed its shores. Life there was consequently much harder, and in the course of the next four centuries these Viking settlers disappeared as a separate racial entity, becoming merged with the Eskimos, whose nomadic existence they were forced to emulate as the only means of survival when contact with the Scandinavian homeland was finally broken.

ACCORDING to the Icelandic sagas, the discoverer of America was Erik's son, Leif Eriksson. It is impossible to be certain about dates and details, for the sagas were not recorded until centuries after Leif's landing. But it is believed that at the end of the 10th Century, Bjarni Herjulfsson, blown off course on a voyage from Iceland to Greenland, made a landfall on a coast that may have been America. Sailing the same boat, which he had bought after Bjarni's return, Leif and a crew of 35 retraced Bjarni's course and reached land, probably Baffin Island, which he called Helluland (Stone Land). Steering southward in search of ice-free inlets, he reached what was probably Labrador. He called it Markland (Forest Land).

Finally he reached a fjord where the sagas say salmon were bigger than the Greenland salmon, a land where there was grass all winter and wild grapes grew. Leif called this Vinland. It may have been Chesapeake Bay, but more likely it was the New England coast. His brother Thorvald then sailed directly to Vinland. He was killed there in a fight with the Indians after a stay of one year. About the same time, Thorfinn Karlsefni, an Icelandic trader, set sail from Greenland with three ships and 160 colonists to establish a settlement on the American coast. They reached Vinland, via Helluland and Markland, and were there three winters trading with the Indians. But when their trade goods ran out, they were forced to retreat, and that is the last heard of any serious attempt to settle Vinland.

There are some indications that Greenland ships sailed to America for timber, but no hint exists of any organized penetration of the country for almost four centuries. By 1262, after Norway had obtained sovereignty over both Iceland and Greenland, Bergen ships had come to monopolize the Greenland trade. Finding it unprofitable, the Norwegians allowed contact with the Greenlanders gradually to lapse until around 1355 when a royal emissary named Paul Knutsson, commissioned to determine whether they had become lax in the practice of Christianity, was dispatched with a fleet to Greenland. The colonists had disappeared, and Knutsson pushed on to Vinland in search of them. And here we come to the most incredible of all the Viking relics—the Kensington Stone found acting as the threshold stone of a Minnesota homestead in 1898. The inscription in runic, the angular alphabet of the northlands, reads: "We are 8 Swedes and 22 Norwegians on an exploratory journey from Vinland through the West. We had camped by a lake with two islands one day's journey north from this stone. We were on the lake and fished one day. When we came home we found 10 of our men red with blood and dead. Ave Maria, save us from evil. We have 10 of our people by the sea to look after our ship fourteen days' journey from this island, in the year 1362."

THIS stone, now returned to Minnesota, was for a time exhibited in the Smithsonian Institution in Washington, D.C. It would be pleasant to believe in the Kensington Stone; alas, no Scandinavian archeologist will accept the too wordy inscription as a genuine relic of Knutsson's voyage. But the possibility that it was inscribed by the homesteader, who knew runic and was a student of Viking exploration, does not alter the fact that the Vikings were in America long before Columbus and that it is generally thought likely that they would have penetrated into Hudson's Bay in search of seals, walrus and skins centuries before the English explorer Henry Hudson gave it its name.

This westward thrust is, however, only part of the almost incredible story of Nordic expansion. Swedish Vikings, reaching southeast and east, achieved something quite as fantastic as the Norwegians and Danes. Sailing across the Baltic to what is now the Soviet Union, they took their vessels up the Dvina River and down the Dnieper to the Black Sea, knocking at the back door of the failing Eastern Roman Empire and threatening Byzantium. They established great settlements at Staraya Ladoga and Novgorod in Russia. By way of the Volga they reached down into the Caspian Sea, crossing it to meet the Arabian caravan routes to Baghdad.

How did they get there? The story is surely one of the most extraordinary of early exploration. They took their boats with them from one river to another, manhandling them across each height of land on log rollers cut from the forest timber. While the discovery of the western ocean limits was often incidental to sailing, a matter of being blown off course, this persistent and premeditated attack on a continent shows the mercantile instinct of these people at its most determined. They were traders, not marauders, and the settlements they built up were trading posts, established for the sale and shipment of a myriad of goods—among them slaves, silks, spices, brocades, jewelry and furs. They opened up the hinterland of Russia for much the same reason that the Hudson's Bay Company and the Northwesters moved into Canada some eight centuries later.

These merchant adventurers in fact penetrated as far into the continents of Europe and Asia as their western Viking brethren traveled across the Atlantic. The very name Russia is derived from them, for they were known as the Rhos or Rus. The word applies only to the Swedes in Russia, not to the Swedes in their homeland, and the theory is that it derived from the word *rodr*, the rowing road.

THE road was rowed with astonishing speed. In 839 Louis the Pious, son of Charlemagne, received an embassy from the Byzantine emperor that included men of Swedish origin calling themselves Rhos. They gave the title *chacanus* to their ruler, the word used by the Khazars and the Bulgars of the middle Volga regions and also by the Arab historian Ibn

Rustah, who wrote of the Rus a century later.

By 941 the Rus, centered on Kiev, were in such force that they could come down the Dnieper and attack Constantinople with (according to one account) 10,000 ships. Their leader was Igor, descendant of Rurik, traditional founder of the dynasty which ruled Russia until 1598. The attack was unsuccessful, but Igor returned three years later to levy taxes.

BY the middle of the 10th Century, the names of the Viking leaders had already taken on a recognizably Russian flavor, and the Vikings were being influenced by the culture of Christian Constantinople. Svyatoslav, Igor's son, refused to adopt the Christian faith. But after his death his son Vladimir became a convert in 988; a little matter of 300 concubines in Vyshgorod, 300 in Bjelgorod and another 200 in Berestovo being apparently conveniently ignored. Vladimir's son Yaroslav married the daughter of King Olof Skötkonung of Sweden and became father-in-law to King Harald Hardrada of Norway, Andrew I of Hungary and Henry I of France. Thus the interconnection of the ruling houses of Europe was projected into Russia at an early date.

Traders, colonizers, explorers, America discovered and a Russian dynasty established—all by the end of the Ninth Century! But the fascinating story of Viking expansion had another side to it, one that was to have an extraordinary impact on the historical and racial background of the English-speaking peoples. It began with the collapse of the Frankish Empire. Louis the Pious had been so successful in reorganizing the sea defenses of Charlemagne's territories that between 814 and 833 the Vikings, whose trading instincts demanded a profit on all piratical voyages, made only one major attack on the continent of Europe—and it was unsuccessful. But in 834 they attacked the rich trading city of Dorestad in what is now the Netherlands and found it undefended, proof that internal dissensions associated with the succession to Louis' throne were weakening the Franks. It was the signal for which the hosts had waited.

From that moment raid followed raid. They struck at Rouen and Quentovic, the two other major trading cities, and attacked Nantes in 843. At Nantes, however, the Danes did not plunder and sail; they stayed the winter.

It was the beginning of the wintering hosts that came to plunder and remained to cultivate. The squabbles of the sons of Louis the Pious, who had died in 840, over the division of the Frankish lands provided the Vikings with easier money than that obtained from plundering, which had become increasingly perilous and profitless. The new source of revenue was the Danegeld—protection money extracted in return for a promise not to attack. Between 845 and 926 a total of 13 Danegelds was levied on the Franks. During this period a new type of Dane had begun to arrive, men seeking land rather than cash. Their leader's name was Rollo, and within two decades this land-hungry Norseman held all northern France under the name of Normandy. Here, on these north-facing Channel shores, was born the power that was to conquer England for the last time in its history.

AT this point it is necessary to take a look at what was happening on the other side of the Channel. The raids on southern England had begun in 835. By 851, there were 350 Danish ships anchored in the Thames. The Danes burned London and Canterbury and wintered in the Isle of Thanet. In 867 they were deep in Northumbria in the north of England; two years later Edmund, last of the kings of East Anglia, farther to the south, was martyred for refusing to renounce his Christian faith. All the great abbeys and monasteries were sacked; one Viking gloried in the fact that he had slain 84 monks with his own hand. By 870 all England north of the Thames was in Norse hands. Wessex, farthest south of the English kingdoms, alone remained free.

As has happened so often in English history, the hour produced the man—Alfred, youngest of the sons of King Ethelwulf of Wessex. The year was 871 and the Danes were swarming into Wessex at last. Leaving his last remaining brother at his prayers, Alfred marched to meet the Viking hordes at Ashdown. The fight raged all day. At the end, thousands of corpses strewed the field and the Danes were in flight.

Nothing like this had happened to the pirate Norse since they had begun to ravage Europe. Alfred was then only in his early twenties, and Ashdown only one of eight battles he fought in 871. That year his brother died. As king, Alfred bought time with Danegeld, and while the Norsemen were partitioning the Midlands and the north, he was reorganizing the whole structure of his kingdom. He formed an elite body of his thanes, the landowners who owed him military service. He set up a navy, reorganized the militia called the fyrd, and fortified strategic towns—the burghs. The massed power of the Danes, augmented by fleets from Ireland and even France, failed to crush him in 876. But in the following winter, the pressure became so frightful that Wessex cracked and Alfred was forced to flee to the Isle of Athelney.

Alfred's greatness lay in his political acumen and scholarship rather than his more obvious military ability. Defeating the Danes in 878, he sought not revenge but friendly relations and by this act of magnanimity, confirming the Danes in their hold on the north, he laid the foundations of English crown and state. He laid the foundations also of English sea power, building ships to meet succeeding hordes in their own element, and in so doing he protected the whole country, Danes and Saxons alike, welding them into one. It was a monumental achievement and when, toward the end of his reign, the Viking hordes battered at his gates again, they were forced to withdraw, frustrated after four years' profitless raiding.

WITH the death of Alfred in 899, the defenses of England slowly fell into decay; nevertheless it was a hundred years before Viking raids began again in earnest. By then the country was rich in culture and wealth, for the Danes, like the Saxons before them, had proved good settlers; poetry, literature and scholarship flourished, monasteries had been rebuilt, craftsmanship encouraged. It was almost a golden age. But the country lacked leadership, and across the seas the Norse were consolidating. Waves of new raiders coming out of the north found continental Europe too tough a nut to crack. They turned once more to England.

After a series of probing raids, they struck in force in 991. The English king was Ethelred, known as "the Unready" for sound reasons. The Anglo-Saxon Chronicle complains: "When the enemy is eastward, then our forces are kept westward; and when they are southward, then our forces are northward." Ethelred died and Edmund Ironside succeeded. He fought five brilliant battles in the year 1016 and then was defeated by the Danish Viking, Canute. Edmund died shortly afterward and the witan, an assembly of king's counselors, in desperation named Canute king.

Canute could have changed the course of history. In 1019 he succeeded to the crown of Denmark; in 1027 he extended his dominion over Scotland and the following year over Norway. He died in 1035, ruler of a great northern empire. Had Canute lived longer, England, Denmark and Norway might have been welded solidly into one bloc. But at his death his witless sons split his domains and the vultures prepared to pick the rich carcass.

IN the year 1066 Edward the Confessor, Canute's ultimate successor, died. The choice of Harold, son of the great Earl Godwin, as successor to Edward's kingdom gave the long-awaited signal to the predators. The fleets gathered—at the mouth of the Dives on the French coast, where William, bastard son of Robert, Duke of Normandy, waited for a southerly wind; in the Norwegian fjords and the Scottish islands, where the Norwegian king, Harald Hardrada, in alliance with Tostig, the English Harold's traitorous brother, massed his forces; off Flanders, where Tostig himself sought men and arms.

Harold's defense of England is an epic of marching and countermarching. Manning the Sussex and Kent coasts through the summer of 1066, he saw his fyrdmen gradually drift away as harvesttime approached. It was September when news came that the forces of the Norwegian king had sailed. King Harald's men broke into Yorkshire, laying waste the countryside the way the early Vikings had, and the English Harold, with only his house carls—the elite royal guard—left, marched north the length of England. He struck Harald's force seven miles beyond York, routed the Norwegians, killed Harald Hardrada and the traitor Tostig, and in the evening chased the remnants of the enemy host 12 miles back to their ships.

TWO days later Harold's men were marching south, back down the length of England again to come within an ace of winning a double victory. The wind had turned southerly at last. William had sailed with a thousand ships and a Norman host augmented by half the adventurous riffraff of Europe, every man intent on carving a niche for himself in the rich, ripe land of England. On October 14 the forces met on a ridge now called Battle, and there by a ruse William of Normandy defeated Harold's house carls when the day was almost lost. The English king was killed by an arrow in the eye. William, the descendant of Vikings, became the Conqueror instead of the Bastard. England was his—no longer Saxon England but Norman England, and Norman rule was not to be light. "Cold heart and bloody hand now rule the English land," a poet reported. But the Normans finally gave the country internal peace, a state thoroughly organized and absolute immunity from further Viking depredations.

Thus in the end the rapacious Vikings faded into the history of other peoples. Their expansion was a brutal one, but the recollection is overlaid in retrospect by their achievements. Like the English of a later period, they were merchant adventurers on the grand scale, and it is this, as much as their fearlessness as seafarers and explorers, that gives the Viking Age its memorable place in the history of the peoples of Europe.

Witnesses to a bloody era, stone columns from which early Baltic traders hanged their enemies stand at Visby on the island of Gotland.

Fierce Conquerors in a Brawny Epoch

If Scandinavians today are peaceable, using their energy for the public good, their ancestors were among the most feared men of the sword that the world has ever seen. First in small bands and then in large disciplined striking forces, the Vikings completely subjugated a good part of France and England and pillaged and terrorized much of the rest of the then known world. Little enough remains of the Vikings' impressive and warlike culture, but what there is conjures up visions of brawny, bearded warriors of the sea braving death for plunder and power.

FORTIFIED CAMP excavated in Denmark once enclosed barracks for about 1,200 men. It was probably used to maintain order in the homeland while the Vikings were attacking England.

Stones arranged in the shape of a ship 50 yards across mark a spot in

BURIED BOAT unearthed at Ladby, Denmark, in 1935 is at least 1,000 years old. A Viking chief's tomb, it held his arms and treasures and the skeletons of his hunting dogs and horses.

Sweden sacred to a Viking cult. The Vikings also left boat-shaped graves.

ANCIENT MEMORIAL, a tall stone engraved with primitive runic writing still stands bleakly where it was raised nine centuries ago by three Viking brothers to honor their dead father.

STARK REMAINS of the conquering Vikings illuminate their customs, faith and highly organized military machine

RUGGED SHIPS have been close to the hearts of Scandinavians throughout history

ORNATE STERN adorns a Viking boat dug from the wood-preserving soil of Norway. The boat now stands in the Hall of the Viking Ships in Oslo. Built in the Ninth Century, it may have been a chieftain's pleasure craft.

JUTTING RIBS of a large 17th Century Swedish warship recently raised from the bottom of Stockholm harbor are constantly sprayed with water and chemicals to prevent the long-submerged wood from disintegrating.

3

A
Struggle
toward Unity

TURMOIL and disruption rent Scandinavia for centuries. Its history is replete with internecine squabbles, dynastic struggles and interminable conquests and counterconquests. Yet through the years an ideal of a united Scandinavia has persisted. In January 1949, with the cold war between East and West just beginning, Sweden suggested a Scandinavian defense alliance based on neutrality. The proposal had considerable appeal. Neutrality had served Scandinavia well in the period prior to World War II, and the alliance almost came into being—despite the centuries of war and despite the fact that the countries of Scandinavia had not been closely joined since the breakup of the Union of Kalmar.

The Union, a stroke of political genius on the part of a great Danish queen, Margrethe, brought Denmark, Sweden and Norway under one crown in 1397. It lasted 126 years and it represented the peak of Danish power and influence. Under Margrethe and her successors, the Kalmar Union stretched from Finland, then a part of Sweden, to Greenland, a powerful alliance of Atlantic and Baltic power that was primarily directed against the growing influence of the north German commercial towns, which by then were already joined together into a mercantile alliance called the Hanseatic League.

It was in fact the strangle hold that the German towns were placing on Sweden and Norway that helped Denmark to absorb both of them into the Union of Kalmar. German merchants in control of the grain trade had come to dominate Norway's economy, thus destroying the financial foundation necessary to the maintenance of the country's independence. And in Sweden, wrangling among the nobility had led to the establishment of a German king, Albrecht of Mecklenburg, on the Swedish throne. Denmark, opposing the dominant Baltic power, believed that only the combined power of all Scandinavia could effectively challenge the Hanseatic League. The symbol of Danish resolution remains to this day, the Goose Tower at Vordingborg, part of the fortress of Queen Margrethe's father, King Valdemar Atterdag. From its summit a golden goose faces Germany, screaming defiance.

Dynastically, Margrethe was in a strong position. She had married Haakon VI of Norway in 1363. Their five-year-old child Oluf had succeeded to the throne of Denmark in 1376, after the death of his grandfather Valdemar Atterdag, and to the throne of Norway in 1381, after the death of his father. As regent Margrethe ruled both countries. In 1386, a year before young King Oluf's death, the Swedish nobles asked Margrethe's help in removing Albrecht of Mecklenburg from Sweden's throne. With their support, Margrethe's troops invaded Sweden in 1389 and deposed Albrecht. Margrethe became the acknowledged ruler of Sweden, as well as of Norway and Denmark. To consolidate her triumph, she had her great-nephew Erik of Pomerania crowned king of all

---

UNIONS AMONG THE NATIONS

DENMARK

The Kalmar Union united Denmark, Norway, Sweden and dependent territories from 1397 to 1523, when Sweden (with Finland) broke away. Denmark lost Norway in 1814 and gave up its sovereignty over Iceland in 1944.

NORWAY

Part of the old Kalmar Union, Norway remained under the Danish crown until 1814, when it was ceded to Sweden. Allowed its own constitution by Sweden, it attained independence in 1905.

SWEDEN

With Finland, which it had conquered by the late 13th Century, Sweden belonged to the Kalmar Union until 1523. It lost Finland (to Russia) in 1809, but ruled Norway from 1814 until 1905.

---

three countries. The ceremony was held at Kalmar, close to what was then the Danish border and the most important town in southern Sweden. The aftereffects of this Scandinavian union were to last for centuries. Norway remained subject to the Danish crown until 1814, Iceland until 1944. Greenland and the Faeroe Islands remain Danish to this day.

But the marriage of convenience between the eastern and western halves of Scandinavia proper was of relatively short duration. Erik of Pomerania did not have Queen Margrethe's genius, and when she died in 1412 the rift began to open. In 1523 Sweden left the Union, and two separate Nordic powers—Denmark-Norway in the west, Sweden-Finland in the east—came into existence. Thereafter, for almost three centuries, Scandinavian history was bedeviled by rivalry between the two.

Denmark was to follow the general pattern of European history. Far more than the other Scandinavian countries, it was exposed to the winds of social and political change blowing through the western continental countries. Although the balance of power was shifting in Sweden's favor, such was the legacy of Denmark's earlier strength that in 1611 it succeeded in briefly capturing Sweden's two strongest frontier fortresses—Kalmar and Älvsborg. But this was Denmark's last serious attempt at Scandinavian hegemony.

Sweden was soon to assume full dominance. In 1621 a great Swedish king, Gustavus Adolphus, having remodeled his army to produce a unique force of conscripts that with Scottish and German mercenaries was eventually to total some 40,000 troops, crossed the Baltic. It was the start of a Swedish expansion southward and eastward into Poland and Prussia, in the course of which Gustavus Adolphus was accused of wanting "to drink up the entire Baltic." To support the conflict, which was part of the Thirty Years' War then raging through Europe, Dutch skill and capital were employed in the development of Sweden's mining and metallurgical industries.

Step by step during the first half of the 17th Century Denmark was pushed back, and when peace was signed in 1648 it was the Swedes who held a Baltic empire, their forces so far west on the north German coasts that they faced the Danes across the Holstein border. Then, in two sharp wars between 1657 and 1659, Copenhagen was besieged, and in the settlement that followed Denmark had to cede to Sweden the northern provinces of Skåne, Halland and Blekinge across the Sound that today separates the two countries. Norway, still under Danish control, lost Härjedalen, Jämtland and Bohuslän to Sweden.

Thus the present borders between the three Scandinavian kingdoms were more or less finally established. The power of Sweden became so great that the Dutch withdrew their support, allying themselves with Denmark in an attempt to preserve the balance of power. The aid of the Dutch fleet saved Copenhagen and prevented both sides of the Sound from becoming Swedish.

The Dutch benefited enormously from these wars, gaining control of virtually the entire Baltic trade. Denmark was left financially and militarily crippled. But in King Frederik III the Danes found a monarch prepared to overhaul the whole machinery of government. He broke the power of the old aristocracy, introduced uniformity into legislation, finance and local administration, and established a standing army. The Danes were prepared for another round. When Sweden supported France in an attack on

QUEEN MARGRETHE, ruling Denmark and Norway, gained control of Sweden, ushering in the Union of Kalmar.

Holland in 1672, the Danes, hoping to regain their lost provinces, joined the Dutch. After a two-year struggle, the Swedes were saved from defeat at the bloody Battle of Lund only by the tactical brilliance of their king, Charles XI.

It was now that the foundations of a new and fateful era of Swedish military expansion were laid. An absolute monarch, Charles reorganized and strengthened his army, and reduced the economic power of his nobles by appropriating their lands. He died in 1697, to be succeeded by his son Charles XII, whose ambitions were based on a study of Alexander the Great. He was only 15 when he came to the throne and in the 21 years he reigned he brought Sweden closer to disaster than it had been in three centuries.

Charles was anxious to put his father's new armies to the test. Aided by England and Holland, he secured his western front by an attack on Zealand which brought the Danes to terms. Then he crossed the Baltic with 10,000 troops to halt the inroads of Russian power under Peter the Great. This 18-year-old boy met the Russians at Narva and broke an army four times the size of his own. The prisoners alone numbered more than his entire force. He marched on Warsaw and Cracow, and using new tactics that centered around the cavalry charge, defeated the Poles and their Saxon allies at Kliszow. Having defeated Poland and Saxony, and having marshaled an army that was as infused with his personal genius as Napoleon's troops were to be with his generations later, Charles anticipated Napoleon's fatal mistake. He marched on Russia, intent on securing his eastern frontiers by destroying the Russians at their center.

His experience paralleled Napoleon's—an elusive enemy, a lack of supplies due to the Russian scorched-earth policy and one of the coldest winters in living memory. The following summer, 1709, he was in high fever from a bullet wound, and his troops, lacking his brilliance of command, were all but destroyed in the Battle of Poltava. Charles escaped to Turkey where he spent the next five years trying to draw that country into his Russian venture. But taxes, plague and bad harvests played havoc at home. The straggling Baltic empire was crumbling. In 1715 Charles returned to Sweden. Twice he tried in vain to extend his empire westward by attacking Norway, and in 1718, while besieging the border stronghold of Fredrikssten, he was killed by a shot, perhaps an assassin's.

Thus, two centuries of rivalry between the Nordic realms had brought no lasting gains for either. Sweden and Denmark-Norway had been reduced to second-rate powers. Many of their statesmen began to realize that war between the two could only be mutually ruinous. Europe was then on the brink of political and military upheaval—the French Revolution and the Napoleonic Wars. Scandinavia had much to lose by involvement. Norway, in particular, was experiencing unprecedented prosperity. During the 15th

BRILLIANT SOLDIER, Gustavus Adolphus of Sweden led forays into central Europe until his death in 1632.

and 16th Centuries west European demand for Norwegian timber had increased sharply. As the coasts were denuded, the industry spread inland, the logs being floated down to the river mouths where towns quickly grew. German merchants maintained a hold on Bergen for some time after they had lost control of the Baltic, but they held only the trade in grain and fish. It was the Dutch who cornered the timber trade. By the middle 1600s, however, Norwegian ships were beginning to oust the foreigners, and before the end of the 18th Century they were trading between foreign ports.

It was a rebirth of mercantile power which was to continue and grow through the 19th and into the 20th Century. A wealthy town class, many of its members immigrants from Denmark, Germany and Holland, bolstered the growing power of the state. The old feudal system was weakened. Norway was still little more than a province of Denmark, but by the late 18th Century its economic growth had made the break with Denmark only a matter of time.

In Denmark, too, feudalism was giving place in the late 18th Century to an economic system under which free peasants owned their own land. This social revolution was to a certain degree hastened by the European struggles which encouraged the export of Danish agricultural products. In Sweden, the expensive wars of Charles XII and the loss of the Baltic empire engendered equally great internal changes. There was a reaction in the country against monarchial absolutism, and the power in the kingdom gradually passed to the Riksdag, or parliament. In Sweden as well, the old feudal structure was disappearing and class distinctions were becoming less marked. The change proceeded through most of the 18th Century; it went hand in hand with the rapid development of industry and the consequent growth in size of towns and cities.

The 18th Century was an age of growing freedom for all the Scandinavian countries, and as a result they were virtually untouched by the currents of revolutionary thinking that swept Europe in the aftermath of France's bloody revolution. Nor did the Napoleonic Wars immediately affect Scandinavia. The area was too far removed from the main center of disturbance and Sweden and Denmark-Norway, as neutrals, were able to make huge profits in trade. England's increasing interference with neutral shipping, however, led Sweden and Denmark in 1800 to join with Prussia and Russia in a defensive alliance based on armed neutrality. England took up this challenge to its increasing control of the seas and the result was disastrous for Denmark. A year later England's greatest naval commander, Admiral Horatio Nelson, turned a blind eye to his admiral's orders and pounded the Danish fleet into submission.

Sweden switched its policy to one that favored England. The motive was more commercial than military. England was the principal market for Sweden's iron and steel. As England's ally, Sweden was fair game for Napoleon's allies, Russia and Denmark. In 1808 they declared war on Sweden, and Russian troops overran Finland. When the hostilities closed, Sweden was forced to cede Finland, as well as a strip of Sweden itself, to Russia. Swedish territory and population were reduced by more than a third. Blaming the disaster on the incompetence of Gustavus IV, Swedish army officers deposed him in 1809. A new constitution was drawn up and a new ruler, a completely unforeseen choice, was named. One of Napoleon's most celebrated marshals, Jean Baptiste Bernadotte, became crown prince under the name Charles John, thus inaugurating a dynasty which reigns in Sweden today.

Denmark meanwhile had suffered almost as much, for the international situation had become so complex that neutrality was impossible to sustain. With the French armies marching northward in 1807, England delivered an ultimatum that the fleet be surrendered before it fell into Napoleon's hands. The Danes rejected it, with the result that Copenhagen was bombarded again. The fleet was surrendered, and the country forced into the French camp.

Once again Denmark and Sweden were on opposing sides and in the years of war that followed all vestiges of Danish power vanished. The state was bankrupt. After a short, direct struggle with Sweden, Denmark was forced in 1814 to sign a treaty ceding Norway, which it had held for four centuries, to Sweden. But the Norwegian people refused to be handed over. They elected a representative assembly to draw a constitution which, with minor modifications, remains in force today and chose a Danish prince as their king. Sweden, unwilling to give up its prize, attacked. The fighting was, however, quickly halted, and a compromise was reached. Norway retained its constitution but was joined with Sweden under the common crown of the Swedish royal house.

This brief struggle was the last of the interminable wars of Scandinavia. Thereafter the three kingdoms devoted themselves to their internal problems. It was an age of liberalism. By 1850 a liberal constitution, a popularly elected parliament and freedom of the press had been secured in Denmark. At the same time there was an increase in foreign trade and some industrial growth. The Danes were the first to organize an effective labor movement and Danish socialists were instrumental in rousing the workers of both Sweden and Norway. Shortly after the establishment of the trade unions came the founding of labor parties; Denmark's was established in 1878, Norway's in 1887 and Sweden's in 1888.

In effect, the three Scandinavian kingdoms, faced with an era of peace, were turning in on themselves, going through the formative process that was to produce the political, economic and social structures that mark them today. But in 1848, the Danish government's attempt to impose its constitution on the southern duchy of Schleswig produced the first rumblings of yet another political volcano. German nationalists in Schleswig and neighboring Holstein revolted. In 1864, after the Danish government had again tried to impose its constitution on Schleswig, Otto von Bismarck, the Prussian prime

RECKLESS MONARCH, Charles XII erred by invading Russia in 1708. His defeat ended Sweden's epoch of power.

minister, declared war, supported by Austria.

For much of their history the Danes had looked upon their southern frontier as secured for all time against invasion by the great earthwork initiated by King Godfred in 808. The modernized Danevirke was to them what the Maginot Line was to France in 1940, and when the commander of the Danish forces withdrew from this ancient barrier in 1864 without attempting to defend it, the fighting morale of the Danish people crumbled. It is true that as the war went on their soldiers fought heroically against overwhelming odds, but the loss of Schleswig-Holstein, combined with the specter of growing German strength to the south, made the Danes feel that defense was hopeless. Their morale never recovered. Herein lies the key to Denmark's behavior in 1940.

Now it was peace in all three kingdoms, a peace that was to last far into the 20th Century. Railways were being built, industries established. The parliamentary system was consolidated and universal male suffrage introduced. The judicial system was overhauled, and the growth of the universities went hand in hand with a move toward compulsory education. Denmark inaugurated a primary school system as early as 1814, Sweden in 1842 and Norway in 1860. Socially as well as politically Scandinavia was becoming democratized.

But, as in Britain, the growth of democratic thought did not preclude the maintenance of monarchial institutions; although the monarchy was stripped of real power, the three countries understood very well the advantages of a head of state divorced from politics. Indeed, when Norway finally obtained independence from Sweden in 1905, it immediately set up a royal house of its own, giving the throne to Prince Carl of Denmark, who became Haakon VII.

While Scandinavia concentrated on its internal affairs and the development of its resources, Bismarck's success in consolidating the divided German states into one nation produced new alignments of the European powers. All three Scandinavian kingdoms were convinced that they could ride out the gathering storm on a policy of neutrality. This depended less on

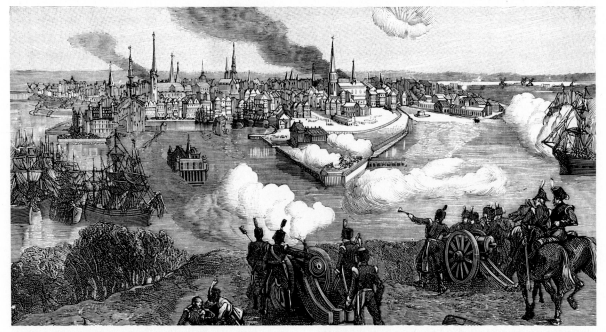

THE BOMBARDMENT OF COPENHAGEN in 1807 was a part of the Napoleonic Wars. To forestall Napoleon's plan to use neutral Denmark's fleet in his blockade of England, the British demanded the fleet be surrendered.

When the Danes refused, the British shelled Copenhagen *(above)* and seized the fleet. Denmark allied itself with Napoleon and in 1814 was defeated by France's enemy, Sweden, to whom it was thereby forced to cede Norway.

their own ability to defend that neutrality than on the intricate balance of power among the nations of Europe. After the storm broke in 1914 their policy seemed justified. True, Norway's merchant shipping losses during the war were second only to Britain's, but as a neutral the country made a fortune carrying for the Allies at war-inflated freight rates. Sweden and Denmark, too, traded with both sides to the great benefit of their economies. And although all three were under great pressure and suffered from the blockade tactics of the belligerents, their wartime experience fostered the belief that neutrality not only could preserve the independence of small countries but could also be made to pay dividends. Indeed, after the war Denmark regained part of Schleswig, which it had lost in the war of 1864, and Norway acquired control of the coal-rich Svalbard archipelago in the Arctic. The scene was set for the tragedy of 1940.

ON April 9 of that year the Germans invaded Denmark and Norway. Both countries were totally unprepared. The illusion fostered by the experiences of the Scandinavian countries in World War I had encouraged them to believe that neutrality was something absolute, that you had only to declare yourself neutral and it would be so.

Sweden had then been free of war for 126 years; so had Norway; and even Denmark had been at peace for 76 years. Long immunity had produced a mood of pacifism among the Scandinavian people. It was as though peace was theirs by right. Norway's Labor government did begin to increase the strength of the country's armaments in 1938, but it was too late.

When Hitler struck, the Norwegian army numbered only 9,000 men. Denmark had called up 32,000 at the beginning of hostilities in 1939, but in 1940 there were no more than 14,000 under arms, barely half of them trained. At the time, it was suggested that the British mining of the West Fjord approach to the iron ore port of Narvik in the early hours of April 8 had forced Hitler's hand, but the first units of

the German invasion had left their home ports as early as April 5. On Sunday, April 7, British air reconnaissance sighted units of the German fleet steaming north. The Norwegian government, several members of which on April 5 had attended a film of the conquest of Poland at the German legation obviously intended to intimidate them, received information from London about the German fleet movements the following day, Monday. No attempt was made to mobilize the trained reserve of 200,000 men. Indeed, while the German armed forces were approaching the Norwegian coasts, the country's parliament debated the mining of territorial waters.

At 4 o'clock on the morning of April 9 the German minister delivered a document declaring that the Germans had arrived as friends to protect Norway against an Anglo-French attack, and demanding immediate surrender. The ultimatum was rejected. The forts guarding the narrows of Oslo Fjord went into action. The German heavy cruiser *Blücher* was sunk and the German ships forced to retire. But airborne troops captured Oslo, and at all other points the invasion went according to plan; Kristiansand, Stavanger, Bergen, Trondheim all fell. Government and king, with the Bank of Norway's gold, retreated inland, taking to the hill country north of Oslo.

THE other Scandinavian country on Hitler's list was given a similar ultimatum, also at 4 a.m. At that moment a German freighter lying at Copenhagen's Langelinie pier was disgorging troops and German forces were crossing the Jutland border. It is only fair to say that the Danish king and his government had no mountains behind them, and that, because of their closeness to Germany, they could expect no aid from Britain. But there was not even token resistance, no attempt on the part of the government to escape. It simply capitulated.

The two kings followed sharply contrasting courses. Haakon was a Dane, but he had been King of Norway for 35 years. On the afternoon of April 10, in the little hill village of Elverum, he reluctantly granted audience to the German envoy, Dr. Kurt Bräuer. Blandishments and threats were met by the simple statement that under the constitution political decisions were the responsibility of the government and the government alone. Haakon rejected absolutely the demand that he should appoint a new government under the Norwegian Nazi party leader, Major Vidkun Quisling.

A few hours later, in the nearby village of Nybergsund, King Haakon faced his ministers in council, a lone man with his mind made up, a rock on which others were glad to lean: "If therefore the government should decide to accept the German demands—and I fully understand the reasons in favor of it considering the impending danger of war in which so many young Norwegians will have to give their lives —if so, abdication will be the only course open to me." He made it clear that he had arrived at his decision after "grave self-examination," that he was not attempting to influence his ministers, but merely stating where his own duty lay. The attitude of the king, which coincided with that of C. J. Hambro, leader of the Conservative party, who had already pledged the support of his party to the Labor government, made the policy of that government in the days to come seem inevitable.

NORWAY fought, all up the length of its mountainous countryside, backed by the British fleet and Allied landings. The struggle continued for a month in the south, for two months in the north. France disintegrated, British support was withdrawn, but units of Norwegians got away across the North Sea and king and government removed to London. Five years of desperate resistance followed, and 40,000 Norwegians were arrested. Some 2,000 of them died, and 336 innocent hostages were executed in a brutal attempt to stop the persistent sabotage. Toward the end of the war all the north of the country was devastated as the German forces retreated before the Russian advance into Norway. Almost 2.5 million tons of Norwegian shipping was sunk, half of a great mercantile

fleet that steamed courageously the oceans of the world in support of the Allies.

Throughout those five years an unending stream of volunteers slipped across the seas to the Shetland Islands and to Scotland in craft of all sorts, even including rowboats, to be trained and returned to their homeland to support the resistance. Their attack on Norsk Hydro's plant at Vemork, whose production of heavy water was vital to Germany's pursuit of the atomic bomb, was one of the most daring raids of the war. In all this great and enduring effort King Haakon was the symbol of national unity and purpose. He died in 1957, mourned not only in Norway but in all the free world, a man of stature and integrity.

DENMARK'S king was Christian X. His prime minister was Thorvald Stauning, his foreign minister Peder Munch. Persistent warnings from their minister in Berlin were ignored. Even the arrival of their naval attaché from Berlin on April 4, 1940, with a report that Denmark could expect invasion within a matter of days, made no impression. The Danish commander in chief's demand for immediate mobilization was rejected.

Semiofficial Danish history deals with the invasion of April 9 very briefly: "Resistance was hopeless, and after a brief struggle the Government yielded under protest, the Germans undertaking to respect Denmark's independence and integrity." The lie that the Germans had invaded Denmark only to forestall the British was publicly supported by Stauning as the year 1941 dawned.

Although the Danes were later to organize a brave and effective resistance movement, only a few men in public life took a stand against the capitulation during the early days. Among them was Henrik de Kauffmann, the Danish minister in Washington. From the outset he refused to accept the authority of either king or government. Since they had not fled the country he regarded them as under Nazi pressure. On the first anniversary of the German occupation of the country he signed an agreement on his own initiative whereby the United States took over the defense of Greenland. The reaction of King Christian was immediate; he dismissed his ambassador. Kauffmann's reaction was equally determined; he refused to accept his dismissal. He was supported by President Franklin D. Roosevelt and there followed a correspondence almost without precedent between king and president. Kauffmann stayed, and when Denmark was finally liberated in 1945 King Christian received him, personally thanked him and officially reinstated him.

How did Sweden react to the occupation of the two neighboring Nordic kingdoms? During the Russo-Finnish war of 1939-1940 it had compromised its neutrality by dispatching large amounts of money, arms and supplies to help the Finns in their struggle to withstand Soviet aggression. It also permitted thousands of volunteers to go to Finland. But when Denmark and Norway were invaded a month after Finland's collapse, Sweden's arms stock was depleted. Had the country entered the conflict it could have expected little help from the Allies.

EXPEDIENCY and self-interest dictated government policy. Shortly after the German invasion of Norway King Gustaf V wrote to Hitler affirming Sweden's determination to defend its neutrality. Three months later, under strong German pressure, the government signed the notorious Transit Agreement. In the face of criticism at home and abroad, the Labor Prime Minister Per Albin Hansson admitted that the document was a concession to the Germans, but refused to concede that it was a violation of neutrality. Yet under this agreement some 140,000 German troops, together with masses of war material, were passed through Sweden for the relief of garrisons in north Norway and thus saved from the risk of British attack on the west coast sea route. In return for the coal and other materials needed to keep its economy functioning, Sweden traded vital war material to Hitler's Germany.

Three years later, when the situation had altered, when first Russia and then the United States had been forced into the war by direct attack, Sweden changed its policy. Instead of Britain's standing alone, a powerful group of allies was everywhere beginning to gain the initiative, and Sweden itself, rearmed and with 600,000 men mobilized, felt it could resist German demands. In August 1943 it halted the transit of German troops and armaments. By the fall of 1944, under increased pressure from London and Washington, Sweden stopped the shipments of ball bearings which had done so much to keep the German military machine running. It also announced that it would not give asylum to war criminals.

AT the war's end, Sweden was rich; Norway and Denmark were both impoverished. Sweden poured out assistance to its devastated neighbors, as well as to the Dutch and the Greeks. During the war it had opened its doors to refugees from occupied Europe and served as an escape route for Allied agents. Nevertheless, feelings against the country ran high. Those who had fought and seen men die in the struggle against oppression could not be expected to look kindly upon their unoccupied neighbor, particularly when they were near to starvation and their neighbor not only was prosperous but gave at least the appearance of having benefited from their adversity.

These feelings are now overlaid by almost two decades of peace. Nevertheless, the marked difference in the wartime experiences of Sweden on the one hand and Norway and Denmark on the other cannot be wiped out just like that. They are a part of history now, and political decisions are to a considerable extent based on history. In the new balance of power—West against East—Scandinavia has had to choose. Norway and Denmark have moved into the western camp, determined never again to be caught unprepared and without allies as they were in 1940. Sweden, with no experience of occupation, its land untouched by war for a century and a half, remains wedded to a policy of neutrality, a kingdom in isolation on the borders between Russia and the West.

TOWERED CASTLE of the Swedish kings, Gripsholm, rises majestically on the shores of Lake Mälaren near Stockholm. Begun in 1537, it was a royal residence until the 19th Century. It houses a large portrait collection.

MEDIEVAL STRONGHOLD, Glimmingehus Castle in Sweden is the scene of a costumed ceremonial procession given by the Guild of St. Canutus. Tall and thick-walled, Glimmingehus was built to withstand long sieges.

Modern Uses for Archaic Institutions

Many venerable institutions still flourish in the old lands of Scandinavia. Castles, some made into museums, form a link with the warrior past. Old churches and universities have adapted to modern times. Royalty, too, survives in these egalitarian and practical nations. The power of these monarchs is severely hedged by constitutions, but they give their peoples a sense of national unity and represent an ideal of domestic solidarity and public usefulness.

CULTURAL CONTINUITY is bolstered by churches and a famous university

INTENT STUDENTS crowd the library reading room at Sweden's Uppsala University. The oldest university in Scandinavia, Uppsala has become a scientific center.

SMALL CONGREGATION celebrates Christmas within the strong stone walls of a 13th Century Swedish church. Ninety-two per cent of all Scandinavians are Lutheran.

STUDENT PRINCESS, Christina of Sweden, in the graduation costume worn at the French School in Stockholm, is given a traditional toss into the air to celebrate the completion of her course.

GYM INSTRUCTION occupies Princess Birgitta of Sweden *(left)*, who studied gymnastics in a state school to earn a teacher's license. Before her marriage in 1961, she taught six classes a week.

FUTURE QUEEN of Denmark, Princess Margrethe *(opposite, in light coat)* listens appreciatively as two men in Viking costume play ancient horns called lures at the opening of a trade exhibit.

SWEDISH SOVEREIGN Gustaf VI Adolf, a respected archeologist and an art collector, posed with the late Queen Louise for this portrait in their Stockholm palace several years before her death in 1965.

NORWAY'S RULER, King Olav *(right)*, a widower, poses with his daughter, Princess Astrid. Olav is a graduate of Norway's military academy and led the Norwegian armed forces in World War II.

DANISH MONARCHS King Frederik IX and Queen Ingrid open an international dairy congress, one of their many official duties. King Frederik loves music and has conducted symphony orchestras.

The Urbane Danes

IT has been said of the Danes that they are the Austrians of Scandinavia. But their gaiety is by no means immediately apparent. Possibly the reputation derives from an earlier period. Less than a century ago Denmark was one of the hardest-drinking countries in the world with an annual consumption of more than two and a half gallons of pure alcohol per head of the population. The Danes still like their *snaps*—indeed, the liquor is considered to be an important corrective to a diet which, with herring in its many forms and large quantities of butter and cheese, is overweighted with fat. But the heavy drinking days have vanished;

taxation has succeeded where in other countries temperance societies and prohibition failed.

It is a fact, however, that the Danes are more voluble, more sophisticated and more in touch with and a part of the world than other Scandinavians. The smallest of the three countries, and the least endowed by nature, Denmark is the closest to western Europe, both physically and mentally. Its capital, Copenhagen, is in every respect a European metropolis. Tucked away at the farthest extremity of the island of Zealand, it is the largest city in Scandinavia, bigger even than Stockholm. More than 1.3 million people live in Copenhagen, more than a quarter of the population of the entire country.

Outside the capital, the countryside also reflects the look of much of western Europe—the people well-fed and contented, the towns and settlements neat, the farms carefully tended, the ports clean and well-organized. The overriding impression is one of orderliness and prosperity. Factories do not obtrude on the gently rolling landscape and there are few big centers of population.

The area of Denmark proper is no more than 16,216 square miles, about half the size of Scotland. Yet it has to support roughly the same population—more than 4.6 million persons—and it is split into fragments by water. Jutland is the only large land mass. This north-thrusting peninsula, sticking out from the continent of Europe like a crooked finger permanently beckoning the other Scandinavian countries, peters out into dunes and sterile areas of peat moor. The people here are different from other Danes and still regard themselves as such—more stolid, more taciturn and sturdy. They refer to themselves as Jyder rather than Danes.

THE little kingdom of Denmark is, like many other nations, an accident of history. To the peninsula of Jutland has been added a conglomeration of some 500 islands, only 100 of which are inhabited. Of these, Zealand and Fyn are the biggest. Bornholm, the most remote, is nearly 100 miles out in the Baltic. Greenland, a land mass of 840,000 square miles supporting a population of fewer than 40,000, was formerly a colony, but since 1953 it has been integrated into the kingdom as a province and now sends two elected representatives to the Folketing, the Danish parliament. The semiautonomous Faeroe Islands, lying almost midway between Scotland and Iceland, also elect two representatives to the Folketing. Iceland, long closely associated with Denmark, loosened its ties after World War I and became completely independent in 1944.

Economically, Greenland and the Faeroes are something of a drain on the country's resources.

Faeroese fish exports (a third of the population obtains its living from fishing) do not cover the cost of imports. Greenland, at one time more or less self-sufficient with its traditional products of dried and salted fish, sealskins and furs, also has an unfavorable trade balance, despite the discovery of important deposits of cryolite, a raw material used in the manufacture of aluminum and other industrial products. Efforts to mine scattered deposits of other minerals have not proved profitable.

ON this cold northern island, where people buy luxury gadgets, even refrigerators, while still living crowded eight to a room, the countless millions of shrimp breeding in the cold depths of Disko Bay on the west coast are a more likely means of financial salvation than the slow progress being made in developing agriculture and industry.

Danish responsibility for the Faeroes and for Greenland in particular, which has been receiving substantial economic and social aid from Denmark since World War II, has thus involved the kingdom in considerable expenditures. Inevitably, the question arises—how does such a small, poorly endowed country manage to look so prosperous?

The answer is foreign trade, the key to the whole economy of the country. The only basic raw materials native to Denmark are clay, chalk and limestone, which are all present in the soil. They are the foundation of the thriving Danish cement- and brickmaking industries and also of the Danes' world-renowned ceramics industry. Other Danish export industries—such as shipbuilding and machinery, and textile and furniture manufacturing—must rely heavily on imported raw materials. In volume, such industrial goods today are rapidly outstripping the traditional export products of the land—grain, sugar beets, potatoes, meat, milk, butter and eggs.

Danish agriculture, however, remains vastly important to the country. A century ago it was considered backward in comparison with British farming, against which it was competing to earn the money for essential imports of coal, iron and manufactured goods. At that time there were about 140,000 farms, many of them operated by tenant farmers. Now there are more than 195,000 small holdings, the great majority of which are owned and farmed by a single family without hired labor. The farms are dotted everywhere throughout the countryside, often screened by windbreaks, for there are few hills to give protection against the prevailing westerlies. Almost half of them are less than 25 acres in size. Another 80,000 or so holdings range between 25 and 75 acres and some 20,000 between 75 and 150 acres. Farms and estates of more than 150 acres number only some 4,000 and account for no more than 13 per cent of the agricultural land area. It is, therefore, the small farmer who is the vital factor in Danish agriculture.

The day for a typical small farmer begins at five in the morning with tea or coffee and a cheese or jam sandwich. At eight he has breakfast—coffee, perhaps porridge, white or rye bread, cheese or cold cuts. He will perhaps have more coffee during the morning. The main meal of the day follows around 12:30: hot fish or meat, with soup in winter and fruit or fruit jelly in summer. After dinner he will normally sleep for at least an hour and then work right through until six or seven in the evening with only a short break about four for coffee or fruit juice. Around six he has a light dinner—more coffee (the Danes are great coffee drinkers and are as fond of cigars as the Dutch) with cold cuts or the lukewarm remains of the earlier, midday meal.

OFTEN the farmer still has work to do in the evening and, of course, the paper work to attend to. It is a hard, exacting life producing little more in profits than a farm laborer's wage, except of course that the farm itself provides most of the farmer's needs, and the profits can be spent or invested according to the inclination of each man.

The small farmer has revolutionized Danish agriculture, pulling himself up by his bootstraps

ELSINORE, a onetime toll-levying town on the Sound north of Copenhagen shown above in an old print, owes its world fame to a fluke: William Shakespeare chose its castle, Kronborg *(far right)*, as the setting for *Hamlet*. No one knows for sure whether Shakespeare ever visited Kronborg. The play is based on the story of a legendary Danish prince, Amleth, who feigned madness in order to avenge the murder of his father by his uncle. In the play, Shakespeare referred to the castle itself as Elsinore.

to make it one of the most efficient in the world. The essential of success has been self-help in the form of cooperatives—cooperatives that are financed by and operated for the benefit of the members. The first credit association was formed as early as 1851. A retail cooperative started by the enlightened Dean Hans Christian Sonne in 1866 at Thisted in Jutland (modeled on one at Rochdale in England) was the forebear of a number of consumer societies, the membership of which now totals 40 per cent of the population.

In the 1880s a sharp fall in the international price of grain led to an expansion in the more profitable export of butter, bacon and eggs. In 1882 the first dairy cooperative was formed by the farmers of Hjedding, also in Jutland. It was so successful that three years later there were 60 dairy cooperatives; now there are more than 800 and their membership totals 163,000, or 85 per cent of all farm owners. Because the whole basis of Danish agriculture is mixed farming, each smallholder or farmer is a member of several cooperatives and frequently of more than a dozen. Thus the cooperative bacon factories are supplied by more than 170,000 producers and the Egg Export Association by 70,000; and there are cooperative societies for the purchase of feeding stuffs and fertilizers, for insurance, even for banking and credit facilities.

In the early days, of course, private businessmen—particularly slaughterhouse owners and retailers—reacted strongly against the cooperatives, but by the end of the 19th Century the movement had gained overwhelming momentum. Now 90 per cent of all milk production goes to the cooperative dairies and to cooperative cheese and butter plants. The 61 cooperative bacon factories, only one of which has been established since 1932, take 90 per cent of all pig production. The dairy farmers themselves stamped out bovine tuberculosis, calling for government intervention only in the final stages of the campaign. This is just one example of what cooperative effort by a mass of small farmers can achieve. In processing, packing and marketing—particularly of the exports Denmark so urgently needs—the cooperatives have given the Danish farmer all the benefits of large-scale production while at the same time ensuring the continuance of the small, personalized farm unit.

THE Danes are very proud of their agricultural accomplishments. After the abolition of serfdom in the late 18th Century, they broke away from the medieval village with its scattered strips of land and established individual, consolidated holdings with the farmhouse and outbuildings the focal center of the unit. Yet despite the fact that the farmers work hard and the agricultural yield is high, the units are still too small for maximum efficiency. The trend now, as elsewhere, is toward the establishment of larger units, but major difficulties are that labor costs are very high and land prices are rising so steeply that expansion is beyond the reach of most small farmers. And, as elsewhere, expanding cities encroach upon the available farmland. Copenhagen is, in fact, slowly swallowing the island of Zealand, and the process will be accelerated if a tunnel or a bridge is constructed across the Sound, and industry and trade become even more concentrated along its shores.

The trend to bigger, more efficient units may, therefore, be accelerated as much by cooperation between small farmers as by purchase. Combine harvesters are frequently seen as one drives through the hedgeless countryside with its white- or color-washed farmsteads, often thatched with ridges of reeds or seaweed scissored in position by split oak timbers like the keel of a ship turned upside down. Although a combine is beyond the financial reach of the majority, several farmers can afford to own one jointly. Such joint ownership is becoming more and more common.

The cooperatives already have begun to adjust to the new trends. Small private dairies and other processing plants are selling out and the cooperatives themselves are merging and enlarging. Ultimately the cooperative units will become really big.

TODAY, Denmark has the highest per capita foreign trade in the world. But the Danes know very well that to maintain that position they must continue to adjust. They are convinced that modern methods will ensure food surpluses in almost all industrialized countries. They are also aware that competition in agriculture will remain fierce and prices low. A further acceleration of the move from agriculture to industry, whose products command higher prices in world markets, is thus inevitable. The Danes, however, come well-equipped to the task, for they have an undisputed genius for marketing. One example: although the country has almost no trout streams, Danish trout have captured much of the American frozen market. The Danes raise the fish in artificial ponds.

A great stimulus to Danish enterprise has been the *Folkehøjskole,* or folk high school. This product of the country people's need brought them into contact with each other and helped them to combine. The folk high schools attempt to whet the appetite for knowledge rather than to give definitive education. The idea of adult education for the mass of the people was first suggested by the clergyman-poet N.F.S. Grundtvig in the late 1830s. The first *Folkehøjskole* was opened at Rødding in North Schleswig in 1844, but it was the one at Ryslinge, started by the educator Christen Kold in 1851, that set the pattern for the system.

THERE are now some 65 of the *Folkehøjskoler*, many of them established in old houses in beautifully landscaped settings. They are mainly coeducational boarding schools with winter courses of four to six months and shorter summer courses. There are even two-week family courses where the children are looked after by trained attendants while their parents attend lectures and discussion groups. The emphasis is on self-education. The majority of the students, who tend to be in their early twenties, today apply for a course for one of two reasons—they are either planning to change their jobs, perhaps from agriculture to industry, or they wish to better themselves in their present employment.

It must be remembered, however, that the schools are not concerned with the techniques of either agriculture or industry. They are concerned solely with the liberal arts, teaching anything from art to history, from languages to English or Danish literature. A student selects six out of some three dozen subjects. There are no final examinations and sometimes students stay on for another term. Although privately run, the schools are heavily subsidized by the government; the fees are low and the lecturers often drawn from among the best-known names in their particular field. The schools project an air of dedication to the arts and to learning for its own sake. The atmosphere is relaxed. The *Folkehøjskoler* constitute one of the most advanced educational devices in the world—and they are entirely voluntary. Their influence throughout Danish community life has been enormous. They have also influenced education in the other Scandinavian countries, as well

---

ICELAND: NATION IN THE ATLANTIC

Under the control or domination of Denmark from 1380 until it regained its independence during World War II, the Atlantic republic of Iceland is Europe's westernmost nation. Icelanders describe their island as "a country of fire and ice." It contains more than 100 volcanoes, plus uncounted geysers and hot springs, but 13 per cent of its land area of 40,000 square miles is covered by glaciers. Situated just south of the Arctic Circle, it nevertheless has a temperate climate, largely because of its proximity to Gulf Stream currents.

GOVERNMENT

The Althing, Iceland's parliament, is the oldest such body in the world, originally established in the year 930. It shares power today with a popularly elected president. Allied with the West, Iceland is a member of the North Atlantic Treaty Organization but has no army, navy or air force. It was one of the original members of the Nordic Council.

ORIGINS

Visited by a number of early explorers, Iceland was first settled by Norsemen in the Ninth Century, many of whom were unwilling to submit to the overlordship of Harald Fairhair, first king of Norway. From 1264 to 1380 the island was under Norwegian control. The continuing stream of immigrants later included families from Sweden and the British Isles. With a population of 180,000, most of it concentrated on the coast, the country remains sparsely settled.

ECONOMY

The country has few natural resources. Farming, fishing and the processing of fish for export are virtually the only industries.

CULTURE

Icelanders speak a language only slightly altered from that which appears in the Old Norse sagas of the 12th and 13th Centuries—which most of them can read without difficulty. They retain a distinguished literary tradition. With a wide network of free schools and a historic esteem for education, Iceland has one of the highest literacy rates in the world.

---

as in Germany, Britain and the United States.

The folk high schools are entirely separate from the normal educational system, which supplies compulsory schooling to the age of 14, augmented by a voluntary system of continuation schools. These include technical, commercial, agricultural, domestic science and art schools. All these institutions, in combination with a public library system with 1,300 local branches and the state-operated radio and television network, have encouraged the process of democratization. In addition, the country's dependence on exports (which means its dependence on factory workers, small farmers and fishermen), plus the taxation policy of successive coalition governments led by the Labor party, has helped Denmark to approach the ideal of a classless society, something which is more of a reality in Denmark than it is in some other highly commercialized societies which have merely switched from a hereditary to a money class structure.

THE Danes, indeed, take equality seriously. Although businessmen can still avoid some part of their taxation, at least there is small chance of favoritism, despotism or corruption in high places. Any person who thinks he has cause for complaint against government officials can take his case to the Ombudsmand, or Parliamentary Commissioner, for investigation. The Ombudsmand is the most highly paid civil servant in the country, and since 1955 he and his office have acted as a safety valve, ensuring the citizen of protection against state injustice. Sweden and Norway have similar institutions.

Apart from its talented people and its productive soil, Denmark has one other very important asset. Split as it is into islands, the country has provided perfect opportunity for the development of water transport. One of the most astonishing sights in Denmark is the shuttle service between Fyn and Zealand, across the Great Belt, where car and train ferries operate winter and summer, gale or calm, in such endless succession that the vessels appear to be on a conveyor belt. In a few years' time, however, the sight may be less impressive; there is a possibility that a tunnel will be constructed under the Great Belt, or it may be bridged, like the Little Belt which separates Jutland from Fyn.

Almost every town of importance in Denmark is a port. This not only means cheap bulk transport within the country, but also a great reduction in the handling charges of exports, which can be loaded onto deep-sea ships within a few miles of their place of manufacture.

At present, Denmark is being plagued with a difficult bout of inflation, a serious situation for a country so dependent on overseas trade. The cause is the same as in many other countries: overfull employment. In the early 1930s Denmark's unemployment rate rose to the incredibly high figure of 31 per cent and even in the postwar period, when many other countries had full employment, the nation had anything up to 11 per cent unemployed. During the past few years this has changed. Now jobs go begging, and almost everyone has money to spend for imported goods. The result is that the balance of trade is in the red. Denmark's National Bank has had to raise interest rates to an unprecedented level. Parliament in addition has slapped on a heavy sales tax in an endeavor to damp down consumer demand. But Denmark is still faced by the well-known vicious spiral in which organized labor, despite its close relations to a left-wing government, presses for increased wages to cover the tax-increased cost of living, thereby defeating the object.

IT will perhaps be difficult to educate the people to self-restraint and to the need to work in harness for the common good. Yet only in this way can Denmark compete in the world markets and keep exports and imports moving through its ports. Many of these harbors have served Denmark for centuries and are, in fact, the basis of its world trade. All through the Baltic one can still see the pitch-black barques, now diesel-driven, that once plowed the oceans under sail. They are now confined to coastal and Baltic trade, but their older crews and men, now wandering the quays in the autumn of their days, eking out their pensions with a little local fishing, will talk of the British ports they once visited regularly, of the United States, Argentina and Brazil.

Svendborg, home port of the early square-riggers, tucked neatly into the quiet of its wooded sound, Sønderborg with its old merchant houses at the exit to Als Sound facing the open waters of Kiel Bay, Korsør, Fåborg,

Aerøskøbing, Kerteminde, Kalundborg—these and a host of others are all thriving ports that have their roots in the past and retain an antique charm. To wander through these old commercial centers or through the smaller fishing ports or through Århus, where workshops and merchants' homes dating back to the 16th Century stand open for inspection, is to acquire a sense of history.

THE sense of peace, of an agricultural community that, while not backward, is still imbued with the atmosphere of the past and the feeling of continuity is felt on Denmark's islands, too. Many of the smaller seem remote, not in distance but in the difficulty of reaching them. These, like Sejrø with its 12th Century, almost Moorish church, whitewashed in the pale translucent light, are the rewards of those who take the trouble to search off the beaten track.

Entirely different is the atmosphere of Copenhagen. Most Danish towns have a pavilion, a sort of dance hall with beer parlor and eatery, where boy meets girl and the family has a night out, all very informal and yet with a clear-cut code of behavior. But only Copenhagen has its Tivoli. The Tivoli gardens, conceived in 1843 by Georg Carstensen, are unique. A mixture of open-air fun-fair, concert hall and bandstand, the Tivoli is full of fairy lights, floodlit lakes and shaded walks, a place of brash amusement and unexpected enchantment with a mass of restaurants that include some of the best in the city. Its attraction is that it appeals to everyone, young or old, rich or poor, low-brow or high-brow. It is, in fact, symbolic, not only of Copenhagen, but of the character of Denmark as a whole, a gay signature tune to the life and mood of a people.

There is only one other part of Copenhagen that matches the frivolity of the Tivoli. This is Nyhavn. A silver thread of the old port running deep into the heart of the city, the canal is lined with bars on one side and merchants' houses on the other, and above the bars are lush apartments. The rich rub shoulders with the purveyors and imbibers of liquor in complete harmony. The atmosphere belongs to the high-living, hard-drinking days of the past; Nyhavn is a part of the city where a sailor coming into this fine port can get anything he wants from girls to dope. He can jive and twist 24 hours a day or lie in a sodden stupor for a week without anybody's denying him the right to do as he wishes.

This is all within a stone's throw of one of the main tourist hotels, and within a few blocks of the royal palace of Amalienborg and the center of government. For the visitor coming to Nyhavn from a tour of the great formal buildings that belong, with their green coppered spires and roofs, to an older, richer period, Nyhavn is a sharp reminder that the sea is the basis of Copenhagen's existence. The capital is a merchant prince's city, with the world its oyster and trade the pearl. The forts that Admiral Horatio Nelson battered, the old gantry for stepping the masts of the great wooden ships of the square-rigger days, the Christiansborg Palace—all the past is still there, pervading the city.

THE present is the result of that past, a continuation of a trading tradition that has increased with the growth of exports and the need for imports. Copenhagen is what London is to Britain, the hub of the country's means of economic survival. The need to manufacture more at home, to convert imported raw materials into manufactured goods for export, only enhances the vital part Copenhagen plays in the Danish economy, and because it is the gateway to the Baltic any improvement in East-West relations, particularly through trade, will inevitably increase the city's importance.

The fact that the Danes are a part of Europe and always have been, added to their worldwide interests, makes them easy for Americans to understand. It is not difficult to feel at home with the Danes. The cold north, to which they also belong, does not obtrude, and the people are friendly and easygoing, with a great appetite for food, for conversation and for culture.

JOVIAL DOCK HANDS indulge in beer, cigars and jokes *(left)* on a quay in Copenhagen's harbor. Carlsberg, a leading brewery, devotes much of its profit to art, science and education.

FESTIVE NIGHT SPOT in Copenhagen *(opposite)* attracts a lively crowd. The Danes consume some 15 gallons of alcoholic beverages per person each year, mostly malt liquors.

An Orderly Land's Cheerful Prosperity

Denmark's well-being, in defiance of a poverty of raw materials, is due almost wholly to planning and hard work. Even those natural individualists, farmers and fishermen, are tightly organized in cooperatives and other marketing alliances. But this atmosphere of determined good sense has not dulled the Danes' natural ebullience. Cheerful in their labor, they love getting together for convivial talk. What might be a dour country rings instead with laughter.

MAKE-BELIEVE GUARDSMEN line up at the entrance of the Tivoli gardens. Made up of youngsters, the smartly uniformed Tivoli Guard marches through the park every evening to the sprightly music of its own military band.

FLOWERY TERRACE of an inexpensive restaurant in the Tivoli gardens *(right)* provides a quiet retreat for family groups and students. Tivoli has 23 restaurants and every kind of entertainment from ballet to flea circuses.

THE TIVOLI GARDENS in Copenhagen form the world's best amusement park

CITY CHILDREN ride in a playpen on wheels near one of Denmark's many fine day nurseries. The state provides all-day care for the children of working parents.

TOWN ELDERS sitting on stones that have been their town's forum for 500 years discuss communal business. Local democracy in Denmark goes back many centuries.

A twisting road winds out of the lonely and forbidding mountains of western Norway toward the fjord-lined Atlantic coast. Called the

Trollstigveien, or Goblin Path Road, it has 11 hairpin turns.

Children of the Midnight Sun

THE pace of life in Norway is slower than in Denmark and much slower than in Sweden. This is particularly true on the west coast and in the north, in Finnmark. Nevertheless, a great deal of work is done, much of it hard physical work achieved in the teeth of hostile elements. The friendliness that a visitor meets everywhere is the friendliness of a frontier people whose nerves are relaxed by physical endeavor. On the coast and in the communities tucked away in the mountains, the people have a childlike quality. There are few neurotics and the suicide rate is very low.

As a people the Norwegians are probably more conscious of the physical nature of their country than other Scandinavians. This is hardly surprising, considering that there are only some 3.5 million of them spread over a land area of 119,240 square miles. Add to this the fact that the distance from its southernmost extremity to Nordkapp in the far north is 1,100 miles, that the length of the coast, including only the larger islands and inlets, is equal to about half the earth's circumference and that no less than 70 per cent of the country is little better than naked rock, and you have the key to Norway's traditional economic problems— a small, widely scattered population and a lack of arable land. The fact that Norway gained sovereignty in 1920 over Svalbard, a group of islands in the Arctic Ocean which includes Spitsbergen and Bear Island, can hardly be said to have added much to the country's natural resources. The islands produce only a little coal. Norway gained even less by later acquisitions —bleak Jan Mayen Island in the Arctic Ocean, the islands of Bouvet and Peter I in the Antarctic and a slice of the Antarctic coast itself named Queen Maud Land after the wife of King Haakon VII.

Norway's productive agricultural land comprises only 2.7 per cent of the country's total area, compared with 73.8 per cent in Denmark which, excluding Copenhagen, supports about the same population. However, nature usually provides compensations, for if it does not, human life, even if it has obtained a foothold, eventually abandons the struggle. In Norway's case the compensations are an abundance of cheap hydroelectric power, the natural raw materials of timber and minerals, and the sea's rich harvest. In addition, revenue from the merchant fleet, third largest in the world, enables the country to balance its trade books. Norway may be poorer than its neighbors, but not that much poorer. Throughout this long country— longer than any in Europe except Russia and only some four miles across at its narrowest— there is a quiet contentment.

ALTHOUGH hard, it is a country of which its people are intensely proud. "In winter the moon is sometimes so bright at midday that you can read a paper by its light." This comment by a resident of Tromsø, a city little more than two thirds of the way up the coast of Norway, graphically illustrates the phenomenon of the daylong winter night. Pilots on the northern run remark on the strange sense of excitement they feel at the first sight of the sun lipping the horizon as they fly south at midday in January; at 6,000 feet or more they know that it will be another month before the people on the ground catch their first glimpse of it. Men will climb mountains on skis to get a sight of what the pilots see, to be reassured that the cycle of the seasons will continue and that the sun will really return.

A PLANE ride north shows the nature of the country more clearly than weeks of land travel. The enormity of the mountainscape is there laid out—the hundreds of miles of snow, glacier, naked rock and forest. Deep in shadowed valley clefts or clinging precariously to the mountain slopes are little patches of green —man's tenuous foothold of cultivation in this hostile land.

The picture is the same along the coast. Behind every inlet, by every isolated fisherman's house lie the terraces of bright emerald green that mean life scratched from a rocky soil. In the center and the southeast rears the forest, with lakes and rivers jam-packed with logs. A hundred years ago 70 per cent of the population was engaged in forestry and agriculture; now the figure is only 20 per cent. The farms are small, usually worked by a single family without hired help.

Only a few years ago the girls would move cattle and goats up to the high pastures as soon as the snows melted, living in the *seters*, or summer farms, while the animals converted the brief, lush summer grass to milk. But that is almost gone now, the *seters* standing empty, the stone walls in ruins, the turf- and heather-thatched roofs falling in. The largest *seters* have been converted into summer hostels for tourist hikers. As in Denmark and Sweden, the small farm is becoming uneconomic and the trend is toward larger units or away from the land altogether. But though there are now some 139,000 farms of more than five acres, there are still at least another 295,000 smaller holdings where the farmer is often also a forester or fisherman. The drift to the towns and industry is as yet less marked in Norway than in Denmark and Sweden, and very much less marked in the north.

The north—Finnmark—seems something of a world apart. Here quite a few people are dark-haired and short, in contrast to the more typical Norwegian, who is tall and fair. The northerners are still so cut off from the rest of the world that the visitor feels himself on exhibit as the inhabitants crowd the quays in curiosity. There are often a few shy Lapps in the group. Of the 20,000 Lapps in Finnmark, many remain followers of the countless reindeer that migrate in herds often numbering a thousand and more; most of them are farmers and fishermen. The fishing, like the hunting, is one of Norway's chief attractions—some 9,000 moose and an equivalent number of wild reindeer are shot annually.

Fishing, hunting, skiing and the midnight sun—these, with climbing, hiking, and car or bus mountaineering, have been made the basis of Scandinavia's thriving tourist industry —pioneered by Norway's shipowners and backed by government agencies. Some two million foreign tourists now pour into the country each year, not counting a further million Swedes who cross the frontier on one-day visits. Before World War II the total of foreign tourists was little more than 220,000.

Some of this increase is due to the success of the government's road-building program. The problems involved in the construction of Norway's 30,000 miles of roads can best be seen on the west coast where highways have to be blasted thousands of feet up mountainsides in dizzying zigzags. The same problems faced engineers building the 2,700 miles of railway. Not only did they have to drive tunnels, but miles of long wooden snowsheds had to be constructed over the tracks to keep them clear of winter avalanches. But still the $90 million or so that the tourist industry brings in barely covers the cost in foreign exchange of the country's own tourists. With relatives all over the world, particularly in the United States, Norwegians are great travelers. The Mediterranean is their favorite vacation area.

Inevitably industrial development has been much more rapid in the south and east where climate and topography make for easier living and communication. But pockets of industrialization have grown up around the mineral deposits and hydroelectric installations of the north despite their inaccessibility. Industry, mining and the generation of power employ almost 40 per cent of the population, compared with agriculture's and forestry's 20 per cent, shipping's 5 per cent and fishing's 4 per cent. Today industry produces about 30 per cent of the national income, five times as much as agriculture, and since the early 1900s the value of its output has more than quadrupled.

Cheap power has been Norway's salvation; Norway is in fact the most hydroelectrified country in the world in relation to its population. It produces more than 30 billion kilowatt-hours per year and it still has a huge unexploited reserve—a potential annual production of 120 billion kilowatt-hours. Like those of Sweden, Norway's new power stations are going underground. Quite apart from the military advantage of having a growing proportion

NORWAY'S TWO LANGUAGES

The Norwegians carry their sense of individuality even into language. When the country was ceded by Denmark to Sweden in 1814, its official language was Riksmål, a Danish dialect mostly spoken by upper class townspeople. Many of the dialects spoken in rural areas stemmed, however, not from Danish but Old Norse, the language of the 13th Century sagas. These dialects had no written forms. While literary figures were urging that Riksmål be made "more Norwegian" by incorporating more Norwegian words into it, a patriotic philologist invented Landsmål, a language based on the rural dialects, and gave written forms to it. Spurred by nationalistic fervor, Landsmål quickly caught on, and the government was forced to make it, too, an official language. Today, both languages are taught in the Norwegian schools, and Norway periodically simmers over the question of changing or modifying one or the other of them.

of electric power safe from nuclear attack, the real advantage of subsurface power stations lies in ease of maintenance, particularly in a harsh climate. In addition, the cost of blasting out the rock caverns and building the inner linings that house the power stations is very little more than it would be if the installations were constructed above ground.

THE underground power stations are very impressive. The station at Mår, just east of Rjukan in upper Telemark, was one of the earliest, having been begun as far back as 1942. The only exterior indications of its existence are massive conduits and a railway track running into an archway in a cliff. Through a tunnel of bare, unlined rock which leads to the turbines, two huge 1,370-yard pipes run down through the mountain at an angle of 40°; the scene is macabre, a perfect setting for a Hitchcock film. Another tunnel, more than 10 miles long, is the main conveyer of water to the plant.

The generator and transformer rooms required the excavation of 61,000 cubic yards of rock. Seen from the control room, the generator room presents a fabulous sight, with five great generators screaming to the thrust of dammed-up rivers high in the mountains above; at the far end the whole wall is covered with a mural map of the catchment area, the region from which the water supply is drawn. And life down here, deep inside the mountains, is no different for the man in the control room or the machine hall than it would be if the station were above ground.

This installation is very much like a dozen others except that some of the power stations are now entirely automatic and the turbine installations in the modern plants are much bigger. Sometimes there is just one generator. Construction of such stations requires enormous technological skills. One example of the blasting expertise of Norwegians using modern techniques is the Spiralen, a two-lane road utilizing six great spirals to ascend the interior of a mountain southwest of Oslo. One would imagine that such a colossal undertaking would

have been constructed only with civil defense in mind; but no, it was built because the municipality required rock for road construction and rather than quarry it in the usual way the engineers blasted something useful.

Norway expects to double its hydroelectric output during the next 10 years. After that, further development of its potential will become more difficult, for the catchment areas will then be in the remoter regions where communications are difficult. Since World War II, development has shifted from the industrial south to the area north of Trondheim on the west coast.

The Norwegians are fond of saying that theirs was the first country to produce industrial products solely from air and water. Hydroelectric power, unlike other power sources such as coal, oil and even uranium, is everlasting— it will continue to serve as long as rain and snow continue to fall. It is the foundation of the electrometallurgical and electrochemical industries. Norway was first to produce industrial

A TRIANGULAR HERD of reindeer moves in typical formation across the snows of northern Scandinavia in this illustration executed about 1907 by a Lapp artist. The lead herdsman *(far right)* guides a castrated male, which is followed by a reindeer trained to follow without being led. This sets an example for the rest. Such sights today are rare; of the 34,000 Lapps, only a small fraction pursue the traditional herdsman's way of life, obtaining their food and skins for clothing and tents from their herds, and eventually selling some animals. The rest of the Lapps, a people who possibly originated west of the Urals centuries ago, have turned mainly to farming and fishing. More than half of them live in Norway, the remainder in Sweden, Finland and the Soviet Union.

quantities of nitrogenous fertilizers from the atmosphere, as it was with heavy water, which is still produced for use in nuclear reactors and biological and chemical research by Norsk Hydro's Vemork installation near Rjukan.

Recent developments in the long-distance transmission of electric power have enabled Norway to build its new industrial plants near the coast, rather than far inland close to the hydroelectric plants. This is particularly advantageous for industries like aluminum, which depend on imported raw materials. Deep-water wharves can be built near the factory sites, and the coastal locations are far healthier for the people, too. There is little sun in the steep inland valleys after the early fall arrives.

Norway's economic and social development was guided by a Labor government from 1935 to 1965. As early as 1903 the Labor party polled 23,000 votes. By 1906 it had 10 out of the 111 seats in the Storting, the country's parliament, and by 1912 it held 23 seats. After World War I the party joined the Third International, the world organization of Marxist groups under the control of Soviet Russia, and was demanding nationalization of almost everything from shipping to banking.

The party's affiliation with Russian Communism, however, involved it in a desperate conflict of conscience—to toe the Third International line meant, in theory at least, abrogating the sovereignty so recently won from Sweden. Martin Tranmael, the fiery leader of the party, refused to accept Soviet dominance, and his party supported him by 169 votes to 103. Thrown out of the International in 1923, the party was free to develop along its own line, and the Communists, split off into a separate party, ceased from that moment to have any effective influence in the nation's affairs—although they did stage a short-lived comeback after World War II. This was partly due to the role they had played in the resistance and partly to Russian popularity in the north—the behavior of the Red Army contrasted markedly with that of the Germans who had wreaked havoc in Finnmark in their retreat before the advancing Russians.

Thirty years of Labor rule saw the party's early ideology greatly modified. Responsibility and experience led to a maturity of outlook and to a lessening of the tensions that bedevil so many other European democracies. The party did not hesitate to sacrifice socialist dogma to achieve practical programs. It did not, for example, nationalize industries, concentrating instead on regulation. The trade unions, too, showed a sense of national responsibility, and for three decades there was no major strike.

The effect of so long a period of Labor government was to accelerate, largely through taxation, the redistribution of wealth and the shift toward a classless society. Ironically, it was just this reduction of class differences that produced a new middle-of-the-road electorate large enough to upset the Labor government. In the fall of 1965, parliamentary control was won by a coalition of four nonsocialist parties—the "bourgeois parties," as Laborites contemptuously called them. However, Labor remained by far the largest single party in the country.

With Labor so strong and closely allied to the trade unions, and with no titled aristocracy to support the royal house (titles were abolished in Norway in 1821), republicanism would appear at first glance to pose a threat to the position of the king. But this is not so. The Norwegian monarchy is eminently secure.

THE man who made it so was Haakon VII. In 1905, he became one of the few kings in history to be elected, not just by the people's representatives, but by the people themselves. Surprisingly, considering that the Norwegians had just broken away from Swedish domination, the Storting first offered the crown to a prince of the Bernadotte family, the rulers of Sweden. When the Bernadottes rejected the offer, the parliament turned to Prince Carl of Denmark, then 33 and married to Princess Maud, the daughter of Britain's Edward VII.

Edward urged immediate acceptance, but Prince Carl—with that determination, that sense of conscience that was to make him one of the outstanding men of his age and one of Norway's greatest kings—refused. He would accept, he told Fridtjof Nansen, leader of the Norwegian delegation, only if the people themselves called for him. Negotiations dragged on until the Storting, finding that its choice had fallen on a man who was adamant in support of his own principles, swallowed its pride; on November 12 and 13, 1905, Norway voted in secret ballot—259,563 for Carl and a monarchy, only 69,264 against. It was a decision that the people of Norway never had cause to regret. Carl reigned for almost 52 years as Haakon VII and in the country's hour of need in World War II he gave his strength to the country he had made his own. In so doing he made the monarchy a vital part of Norway.

BUT it is not only on the memory of Haakon that the position of the monarchy rests. The first and second sentences of the constitution read: "The Kingdom of Norway is a free, indivisible and inalienable Kingdom. Its form of government is a limited and hereditary monarchy." The executive power is vested in the king and he apportions it among his ministers. The king's person is sacred; he cannot be blamed or accused, and responsibility rests with his Cabinet. His relations with the Church are governed by the clause which states that he shall profess, maintain and protect the Evangelical-Lutheran faith, the state religion.

The interesting point about this constitution is that it was passed by the Constituent Assembly as far back as May 17, 1814, shortly after Denmark had been forced to cede Norway to Sweden. Nearly a century was to pass before the new constitution became the effective instrument of a free and entirely independent Norway. Any party which attempted to overthrow this constitution now would find itself immediately in conflict with the Norwegian people, to whom the king is the symbol of their recently achieved independence. However egalitarian the policy of government, Norway without a king is unthinkable.

Folk dancers prepare to entertain at a picnic given by the king of Norway to celebrate a regatta held each summer in Oslo's fjord.

Outdoor Vigor in a Stark Landscape

Norwegians combine the social virtues of 20th Century man with the direct vigor and adventurousness of their Viking forebears. Stable in their home life, they are also ardent seafarers and explorers. Able administrators, they love above all to climb and ski their jagged mountains and sail their cold fjords. Although the Norwegians act like modern bourgeoisie the world over, something about them suggests the rigors of the Arctic, the solitudes of the sea.

ROCK-STREWN SHORE of one of the Lofoten Islands of Norway's arctic north makes a playground for fishermen's children. Offshore ride a few of the island's trawlers.

ORDERLY HOUSES of Narvik nestle on the banks of a deep fjord under the shadow of snow-capped peaks. A thriving port, Narvik transships iron ore from Sweden.

SKIING attracts
the athletic Norwegians
whose many hills
and long winters provide
fine slopes and deep snow

PACKED CROWD watches intently as a ski jumper *(opposite)* flies from the immense chute at Holmenkollen near Oslo. About 100,000 people attend the annual Holmenkollen competition. The Norwegians introduced ski jumping and slalom competitions, both of which have given impetus to skiing's present worldwide popularity.

EAGER BEGINNER, five-year-old Jan Randers *(right)* receives instruction and encouragement from his father, who is the energetic head of Norway's Atomic Energy Council. Norwegians also love skating on their long-frozen lakes, idolize their champion speed skaters and in recent years have developed skills in ice hockey.

6

The Industrious Swedes

A DRIVING energy seems to be a characteristic possessed by almost all Swedes. There is a sense of thrust and concentration, manifested in the way they work, in the intensity of their lives, even in the way they handle their cars. Yet they are conformists, both to the regulations of law and to the formalities of social life. They are considered shy and cold, and fervent only in their love of nature. Visitors find them at their best in the isolation of their country retreats in the forests and by the sea. Isolation, in a geographic sense, has played a role in shaping the character and history of the nation. A knowledge of geographical detail is in fact essential to an understanding of the underlying division, mental as well as physical, between Sweden and the other two kingdoms of Scandinavia.

With a population of 7.5 million people and a land area of 173,648 square miles, Sweden is by far the largest of the three countries. Although broader, it is shaped much like its neighbor Norway, but narrowing only slightly from the greatest breadth of 250 miles. Skåne, its southernmost province, however, extends much farther south, to the same latitude as the border between England and Scotland. Skåne does, in fact, push so far down into the

The Industrious Swedes

Baltic that the ferries plying between Trelleborg and Sassnitz in East Germany make a sea passage of only 58 miles. In the far north Sweden stops short only just above the level of Norway's Lofoten Islands, cut off from all that Arctic Ocean coast by the Finnish and Norwegian borders. The western frontier that divides Sweden from Norway is the great mountain spine that sweeps down the length of the Scandinavian peninsula. Sweden's eastern limits are the Baltic Sea and the Gulf of Bothnia, narrow strips of water on the other side of which are the Soviet Union and Finland.

Internally Sweden is divided into three historic parts. Götaland in the south was the traditional land of the Goths; Svealand, which is the middle section, was the home of the Svear; Norrland (the Northland) supported nomadic herdsmen.

GÖTALAND, which includes the great port and shipbuilding center of Göteborg, is a rich lowland area with a climate tempered by the waters of the Atlantic and the Kattegat. Skåne is especially favored by this climate. Though in area it represents only 2.5 per cent of Sweden, Skåne accounts for 12 per cent of the country's population. It is the granary of Sweden. It was the first area to be settled; here the Danes gained their foothold in Sweden centuries ago. All through the Götaland region can be found the remains of early settlers—the royal grave at Kivik in Skåne dating from about 1200 B.C., the Ninth Century Rök Stone in Östergötland which carries the longest of all of the many runic inscriptions of Sweden and the Bronze Age rock carvings of ships in Bohuslän which are at least 3,000 years old. The towered walls of the medieval town of Visby, on the eastern island of Gotland, still stand witness to the fact that the city was once a great port of the Hanseatic League.

Impenetrable forest once separated the Svear from the Goths, and while the southern people had continental and western associations, the Svear faced east; they were, in fact, the people who pushed their long ships across the narrow seas to Russia in the Ninth Century. Svealand's heart is centered around the island-studded lake of Mälaren; where the waters of the lake flow out into the Baltic the Swedes built their great city, Stockholm. The province of Uppland to the north contains the huge burial mounds of Swedish kings; at Old Uppsala, on the site of a heathen temple, the first Christian cathedral was built; nearby, in modern Uppsala, is the seat of Sweden's oldest university, founded in 1477. In the 16th Century, when the country was attempting to throw off the Danish yoke, it was the people of the northern province of Dalarna who rallied to Gustav Vasa and made the independent kingdom of Sweden possible.

But it is more than historical tradition and the character of its people that give Svealand its present importance. Here, buried in the soil, lies the fount of Sweden's wealth and prosperity—the iron ore on which its industrial power has long been based. Svealand was originally surrounded by deep forest, an unlimited fuel source for the ironworks and of material for houses and ships. It was a priceless heritage. The firm of Stora Kopparbergs Bergslags Aktiebolag, whose wealth rests on the two complementary assets of ore and timber, dates back to the 13th Century. It is the oldest company in the world still operating, forerunner of all the great names of Swedish industry—Bofors, Volvo, Saab, AGA, Bahco, Electrolux, Atlas Copco, L. M. Ericsson, Turbin, Separator, Svenska Metallverken, ASEA and SKF.

NORRLAND, on the other hand, offered little to the early settlers but a waste of forests and mountains that has only slowly and painfully been opened up within the last century. The region constitutes more than half the total land area of the country, and it was mainly the world demand for the products of its forests and mines—it, too, was found to contain important iron ore deposits—that caused the Swedes to penetrate and settle its silent vastness.

Kiruna, a town of some 26,000, is the country's most productive iron mining center. It lies north of the Arctic Circle, not far from Sweden's highest mountain, 6,965-foot Kebnekajse. The iron ore mountain of Kiirunavaara that is the reason for the town's existence can be seen for miles, a wide reddish slash of opencast workings. Today mined underground, Kiruna's high-grade ore is transported by rail past the "Lapp Gate" gap in the mountains to the Norwegian port of Narvik. It was this export route and the demands of the German armaments industry that made Narvik such a bone of contention in World War II, particularly in 1940.

SOUTHEAST of Kiruna lies Malmberget, another productive iron mine with a fantastically intricate network of underground railways. Most of Malmberget's ore is shipped to Luleå, where a government-operated ironworks has been established to provide local employment. Also operated by the government are some of Norrland's great hydroelectric plants, including the huge underground power stations at Harsprånget and Stornorrfors.

Such power stations and iron mines are among the very few nationalized industries. Despite all the talk of socialism, the Swedish government does not normally compete with private enterprise. But in the province of Lappland, as in all far northern areas throughout the world, government financial aid is essential. Here there are some 10,000 Lapps, and about a fourth of them still live a nomadic existence following their reindeer herds, which number more than a quarter of a million. The rest have settled and become farmers and factory and office workers. It must, however, be remembered that the Inland Railway into the far north was completed only 25 years ago. The mood is still a frontier one, the feel of the country not unlike that of the north of Canada.

Norrland's southern provinces are easier of access. Here the proximity of iron ore and other minerals, in addition to the ubiquitous forests, which are of very high quality, has attracted industry. In fact, it was here in Gästrikland, as far back as 1858, that the Bessemer smelting

THE PREVENTION OF DISTRESS

Swedes talk of making their country into a "home for the people," and their social-welfare programs have attracted worldwide attention. There are, in fact, similar programs in Denmark and Norway. Danes speak, in time-honored phrasing, of achieving "the greatest possible happiness for the greatest number of people," and Norwegians of guaranteeing "security regardless of individual success." In no other area of the world are the scope and scale of welfare benefits so extensive as in Scandinavia.

BASIC AIMS

The welfare policy of all three nations differs from that of other countries in its emphasis on the prevention of distress rather than on its cure. In the United States, for example, aid is granted to indigent families with children to prevent the breakup of families for financial reasons. In Scandinavia mothers receive annual cash payments of from $50 to $90 for each child under 16, regardless of the family's circumstances. There are no means tests for any of the important benefits.

MAJOR BENEFITS IN SWEDEN

In addition to the general cash allowance for children, Sweden gives free health supervision and preventive medicines to infants and children up to primary-school age. After that they receive free school medical examinations. Children of low-income families receive transportation to free vacation camps. Books and meals are supplied through primary and secondary school; tuition is free through college. Home-furnishings loans are granted in cases of need to newly married couples and unmarried mothers. Employed pregnant women receive six months maternity leave at two thirds pay. All women are granted free confinement care and a cash payment of $180; those in need can receive supplementary cash allowances. Low-income housewives with at least two children under 15 are entitled to free transportation for annual vacations.

All Swedes belong to a government-administered health insurance plan to which they make modest contributions. Hospital treatment in wards, operations and transportation to hospitals are free. Employed persons receive cash allowances while absent from work. On retirement Swedes can receive free hospital care for 180 days, housing allowances and pensions of two thirds of their maximum annual income before retirement plus supplementary cost-of-living increases.

COSTS

Denmark and Norway spend about 13 per cent of their net national incomes on welfare, Sweden a trifle more. Britain, by comparison, spends about 12 per cent, the United States about 6 per cent.

FUNCTIONING TRADITION

Despite their size, the welfare programs in Scandinavia are conducted with a minimum of friction. Arising out of long tradition, there is in all three countries an attitude of mutual trust in the honesty of both the administrators and the recipients of the aid.

process was first employed successfully. In the 20th Century industrialization has been speeded by the rapid development of timber processing, the mouths of all the great logging rivers being occupied by plants for the conversion of logs to lumber, pulp and packaging materials.

THE transportation of felled timber by water originally gave Sweden a cost advantage over countries using land transportation. Now, however, the long wait for the ice break in the rivers, the resulting seasonal employment problems and the deterioration in the timber's quality after long immersion is causing a shift to year-round road haulage. This has meant the construction of hundreds of miles of forest roads, some of them being real highways on which heavy trucks can move at high speed. The cost of construction is high, but these new roads will also have the effect of increasing the rate at which the northland is opened up.

Farther south, in the more developed areas of Svealand and Götaland, the country faces different problems. Sweden is not exempt from the worldwide shift from country to town brought about by growing industrialization. In less than a hundred years the farming population has decreased by a half. As in other countries, mechanization is taking up the slack. So far the actual amount of land under cultivation has not changed much, but it is estimated that by the end of the 1960s the number of farms, which in 1950 totaled some 300,000, will have fallen to 200,000. The small farmers, who today augment their incomes by working in road construction, or as part-time foresters or fishermen, are now engaged in the process of adjusting themselves to new conditions.

With 75 per cent of the farms less than 25 acres in size the move, as in the rest of Scandinavia, is toward larger, more economical units, greater mechanization and specialization in production—a process, in fact, of agricultural industrialization. The growth and centralization of Sweden's cooperative marketing organizations tend to encourage this shift, as do the high standard of living, high wages and the competition from cheap agricultural imports.

The small manufacturing industries are also growing fast throughout Sweden, side by side with big business. Almost 50 per cent of all factories are workshops employing 10 or fewer workers. These small workshops employ only 7 per cent of the total industrial labor force, but with cheap power at their disposal they provide not only a continuation of the old, traditional metal craftsmanship but also an outlet for the inventive abilities and the creative instinct for design that have always been a source of Sweden's strength.

These small industrial shops are encouraged by the government, for their presence in all sections of industry increases diversification and makes specialization possible. This is important for the development of new ideas in a period when the trend in large concerns is toward standardization of products. The desire for a personal business remains the hallmark of a country where a sense of individuality continues to be strong.

The development of the Swedish system of government, like that of its industry, was influenced by the nature of the country. As with Norway, the isolation caused by topography and climate tended to encourage self-government in the widely scattered communities, making the transition to democracy relatively easy.

THE Swedish parliament, the Riksdag, like Norway's Storting, is composed of an Upper and a Lower House. Sweden has only four major parties—Social-Democrats, Conservatives, Liberals and the Center party, formerly known as the Agrarians. The Communists have few seats. The Social-Democratic labor party has been in power almost continuously since 1932 and like the Danish Labor party it has been mellowed by responsibility. The ability to temper their policies to existing circumstances has been the strength of the Social-Democrats over the years. For three decades the party has ridden a wave of increasing industrialization and high productivity, and it has redistributed much of the resulting wealth throughout the country with the proceeds from high taxation.

For years, incomes have been heavily taxed, as they have been in Denmark and Norway. Also common to all three countries is a tax on net personal assets. These and other levies combine to make Sweden one of the most heavily taxed countries in the world. But because education at all levels is free and social welfare benefits are remarkably comprehensive, most people feel that they are getting good value for their high tax payments.

A REMARKABLE Swedish achievement is the country's solution of labor relations problems. A solution was necessary, for although Sweden may not be in such desperate need of imports as Denmark, it still lacks liquid fuel, coal and many other essentials. In fact, the maintenance of its high standard of living requires imports on a scale that can be balanced only by the export of at least one fifth of its national product. An important step in labor-management relations was taken in 1928, just before the start of the great depression, when an act was adopted legalizing collective-bargaining agreements and a special court was set up to interpret their meaning. If disputes arise over a labor contract, they must be referred to the court, which may impose penalties on the party found to have violated the agreement. Another and even more significant milestone was reached in 1938 when the trade unions and employers' organizations signed an agreement which pledged both sides to close contacts, including joint decisions on the allocation of profits.

Behind this development lay more than 30 years of bitter strife, including a nationwide general strike in 1909. Recent years have been quieter. Sweden's last major labor conflict occurred in the metalworking industry in 1945, when 11.5 million man-hours were lost. The strike was badly timed by the unions, and it was settled on terms not much different from those that were originally offered the workers. In the last few years, Sweden has lost fewer working days because of open labor disputes than any other country with a free trade-union movement. Wages are the highest in Europe, and interunion disputes are rare.

Good labor relations, like the broad extent of welfare benefits, have been achieved only at a price. That price is the rising cost of living. In a world inflationary period the rise was in line with that of other countries. But now it is difficult not to feel that Sweden is in danger of pricing itself out of the world's markets—despite the optimism of Social-Democratic leaders, who point to recent improvements in export sales and the possibility of an increase in productivity. Meanwhile vacations for all are being extended from three weeks to four—one twelfth of the working year. And Sweden, with a low birth rate and a long life expectancy, will in the future face one of the worst old-age problems in the world; the working population will have to support an ever-increasing number of persons who have reached pensionable age.

Other difficulties besides these beset modern Sweden. Because of the climate and the high cost of heating during the long winter months, the emphasis has been on the construction of apartments rather than houses. For the man who spends most of the daylight hours at his job in the company of his fellow workers apartment-living is not a problem, but for the woman, cooped up in close company with the pent-up energy of her children, it adds greatly to the nervous tension of modern life. The problem exists elsewhere in the world, of course, but for Sweden it is greater. Two thirds of the population lives in apartment houses.

S WEDEN'S military isolation has a different kind of impact on its people. The country's leaders have felt compelled to make elaborate and costly defense preparations. The air force, which is currently the fourth largest in the world, has gone underground, burying its fighter and fighter-bomber squadrons in rock hangars from which they can become airborne in a minute and a half. The navy, too, has rock pens for its submarines, its torpedo boats and even its destroyers. Both services are fully equipped with underground maintenance and repair workshops. The radio-communications system is buried deep in the native rock, secure from nuclear attack.

None of this, of course, is visible to the general public. What brings the gravity of the country's exposed position home is the civil defense preparations. Plans exist for mass evacuation of cities. Stockholm has four great subterranean shelters blasted out of the rock. Each is capable of sheltering 20,000 people. These and smaller shelters are in constant use as garages, gymnasiums and restaurants. Every apartment house and modern office block has its own bunker, buried deep in the rock below. Military and civil defense service is recurrent and this, together with the pamphlets covering every eventuality in the case of war, is a constant reminder of Sweden's position on the flank of the Soviet Union.

IN the event of nuclear attack Sweden expects its detectors to give it some four minutes' warning. Four minutes is not much, but Sweden considers that previous political maneuverings will give it time to get its people into their civil defense positions. The country claims that its military organization, based on regional centers, makes it possible for 60 per cent of its army reserves to be mobilized and deployed in six hours. The cost to an aggressor could be very great, bearing in mind the nature of the country and the degree to which defenses, fuel installations and even factories have been buried underground. But the emphasis on the nuclear aspect of a possible war is a strain on the people, living as they must with the feeling that after the thousands of years it has taken man to develop from a cave dweller he is now being forced back into a troglodytic existence.

They will tell you in underground factories that the air is better than in most above-ground works and that workers are healthier. But of the long-term psychological effect of the defense preparations nobody can speak with certainty.

Whatever its strains, Sweden remains a stable constitutional democracy. The king's position is laid down in the constitution of 1809 and its subsequent amendments. It is much the same as in the other two Scandinavian countries—he is bound to accept the advice of his ministers and must choose his cabinet from the party or group that holds the parliamentary majority.

Unlike the Danish monarchy, which in 1953 was opened to female succession, Sweden's monarchy is hereditary for male descendants only. The interrelation with the other Scandinavian countries is strong, both the Norwegian and Danish kings having married Swedish princesses.

KING Gustaf Adolf, who did not come to the throne until he was 68—his father was the tennis-playing monarch, Gustaf V, who died at the age of 92 in 1950—celebrated his 80th birthday in 1962. Admired and respected, he is a man of great culture and learning, with a professional interest in archeology. His apartments in Stockholm Castle are crammed with books, and he has a fine collection of pictures.

As in the rest of Scandinavia the established church is Lutheran. The church suffers, even in country districts, from a wretchedly low attendance. And yet the Swedes could not be called pleasure-seeking, as is immediately apparent to anyone visiting their capital city. Like most capitals, Stockholm is a symposium of national character and background. It is even more a city of water than Copenhagen, but there is not the same lightness of touch. For all its charm, there is a stern formality about it.

Nowhere is this mood more apparent than in the cold vaulted interior of that dark graveyard of Swedish kings—the Riddarholm church. Here is architecture to match the bald, ice-worn rock of the skerries, the dark of the spruce, the cold of countless bays and inlets with water congealing to winter ice. Even the much-loved City Hall, the masterpiece of the architect Ragnar Östberg completed after 15 years' work in 1923, has something of the same atmosphere, its supposedly Venetian quality overlaid with austerity. But in the sparkle of midsummer one finds a lighter touch, the towns bright by the water's edge, the wooden houses grown into the coastal rock. Still, the atmosphere is of the north, the clear light itself reflected in the people.

Near a tall Carl Milles sculpture of Orpheus, the mythological musician, Stockholm residents rest on the steps of the city's concert hall.

A Fast-Paced Nation, Busily Intense

The most industrialized of the Scandinavian countries, Sweden is inevitably the most frenetic. People work hard and the pace is swift. Rivers rush with freshly cut timber; bulldozers on their banks busily build new dams to supply power for the country's homes and factories. With a similar intensity, the hastening Swedes pursue the warmth of the sun. In the brief summer of their northern land, faces in city and country alike strain upward toward the sky.

THRUSTING SKYWARD, a group of 18-story store and office buildings rises beyond a temporary overpass in midtown Stockholm. Planned with the aim of easing congestion, each building has underground floors for parking and deliveries. Trucks and cars reach them by tunnels and overpasses on which no stopping is allowed.

DRIFTING IDLY, logs float by a sawmill on a river southwest of Stockholm. Some 30 per cent of the country's overseas trade is made up of forestry products.

CLEARING GROUND, bulldozers work on the new Messaure Dam in northern Sweden. The Swedes are among the leading producers of hydroelectric power in Europe.

WELL-TENDED PATIO of a worker's home in Kiruna, the Arctic Circle city which is Sweden's largest iron-mining center, draws a mother and daughter into the summer sun. Kiruna's summer is short, but wages paid by the LKAB mining corporation are among Sweden's highest, and rents are moderate in company housing.

AT BREAKFAST Harry Löfquist, a steelworker for the Grängesberg Company in Oxelösund, sits with his family in their three-room, partly company-financed apartment.

AFTER WORK Löfquist helps his two boys, Hans, 15, and Stig, 12 *(below)*, with their homework. Grängesberg provides inexpensive medical care for workers' families.

IN THE PLANT Löfquist takes a coffee break. He is a shift foreman, earning about $400 per month. The national average salary for such foremen is $350 per month.

ARRIVING HOME, Gunnar Engellau, managing director of Volvo, Sweden's biggest auto manufacturer, springs from a Volvo sports car designed for the U.S. market.

TELEPHONING from a hall in Volvo's plant at Göteborg, Engellau finds privacy in a plastic booth he designed. He normally spends 13 hours a day on company affairs.

TOURING the assembly line *(left)*, Engellau checks a schedule. Since he took over in 1956, Volvo's output has climbed from 36,766 cars a year to almost 80,000.

AT A REUNION, Engellau gathers with his wife Margita *(far right)* and six children. When he took the Volvo post, he warned: "I have my family and I'll not give up family life." But such well-attended meetings with the children are rare. At Engellau's urging all have studied abroad, or will; son John-Jacob is an engineer in Paris.

7

Personalities
of
Peace

ON September 18, 1961, a DC-6 crashed a
few miles north of Ndola in Northern
Rhodesia. On board was Dag Hammarskjöld,
the Swedish Secretary-General of the United
Nations. There were no survivors. It was a
tragedy that, like the whole Congo situation,
stemmed from hasty decision, for the flight
was an improvised one. Hammarskjöld had
been Secretary-General for eight years, since
1953. He had gone out to Africa in a final effort to reach a settlement of the long struggle
between the disordered Central Congolese Government, which he had backed through the
United Nations, and the copper-rich province
of Katanga. The Congo was very much his
problem, and the chaos that followed the pre-
mature departure of the Belgians who had so
long held the area as a colony, the subsequent
massacres of Europeans and the collapse of all
civil order and military discipline provided a
great test of United Nations policy.

At the time of Hammarskjöld's death, the
Swedish prime minister, Tage Erlander, wrote
of him: "A devotion to duty, sharp intelli-
gence, objectivity and scrupulous honesty have
been the hallmarks of Dag Hammarskjöld's
tenure of office as Secretary-General. In this he
has lived up to the highest expectations. But

the essential in his life's work was, nevertheless, something beyond this, namely his determined will to create an international organization with authority and power to act. The United Nations' intervention in the Congo became for him the touchstone of the United Nations' ability to create peace and stability." It was, in fact, Hammarskjöld who had insisted that the United Nations be assigned a military force with which to implement policy and preserve order in those parts of the world which were likely to become inflamed.

BY insisting on giving teeth to the U.N., Hammarskjöld was moving beyond what many of its founders had originally conceived to be the purpose of the organization. In fact, when the Norwegian Trygve Lie was elected the first Secretary-General in 1946, the choice was undoubtedly based on the aura of neutrality that had come to be associated with the Scandinavian countries. Lie was regarded as a safe choice, acceptable to East and West. He was a lawyer who had moved into politics through the Norwegian Labor party. At the time of the German occupation in World War II he escaped to England to become foreign minister in the government in exile. He was chairman of the Norwegian delegation to the United Nations conference in San Francisco in 1945 and also of the committee that drafted the organization of the Security Council.

First Trygve Lie, then Hammarskjöld; for more than 15 years these two Scandinavians in a sense were the United Nations. It was they who molded it, although Dag Hammarskjöld's influence was by far the greater. At the time of his death he wielded extraordinary power in the field of international politics and his personality and outlook had permeated the whole permanent staff of the U.N.

To understand how and why these two Scandinavians should have come to have such influence in international affairs, it is necessary to have a clear picture of the world image created, whether intentionally or not, by the countries of Scandinavia. It is this image that made the choice of a Scandinavian as the first Secretary-General a natural, almost inevitable one. Norway, in particular—a country that had suffered greatly under the German occupation and one devoid of any worthwhile overseas possessions or any pretensions to world power—seemed possessed of all the qualifications to provide United Nations leadership.

The image a country, or bloc of countries, creates for itself is partly the result of the political expression of its people and partly the behavior and record of its public figures, particularly those who have achieved international fame. It is with the public figures that we are concerned in this chapter—the personalities that have done so much to express Scandinavia's desire for peace; to fix, in fact, that image in the public mind throughout the world.

One of the most fascinating of these personalities was Alfred Nobel. The Nobel Peace Prize, together with the four other awards for work in physiology or medicine, physics, chemistry and literature, is undoubtedly the most publicized of all international awards. The awards were first made in 1901. The literature and science prizes are given by various Swedish institutions. The Peace Prize itself is awarded by a committee chosen by the Norwegian Storting. At the time the awards were established Norway was united with Sweden. Nobel himself was a Swede.

NOBEL was a strange, misanthropic, unhappy man who, as a chemist, utilized nitroglycerin to create the more stable explosives dynamite and ballistite. He girdled the earth with a chain of high-explosives factories which, at the time of his death in 1896, had made him one of the world's richest men. Nevertheless, his was the loneliness of the idealist whom life had thrown to the wolves. In the latter part of the 19th Century, explosives seem to have had the same fatal fascination as gold for the shadier members of the human race, and Nobel met more than a few of them. "You refer to my many friends," Nobel wrote. "Where are they? On the muddy bottom of lost illusions, or busy listening to the rattle of saved pennies."

Fortunately for Alfred Nobel he never lived to see the havoc his new smokeless explosives wreaked on the battlefields of Europe between 1914 and 1918. Was it the premonition of this that made him devote so much time and energy to considerations of peace? No doubt he had some glimmering of the gathering storm when on November 27, 1895, just over a year before his death, he signed the famous will that was to establish, after some four years of controversy, the Nobel Foundation.

NINETY per cent of Nobel's fortune was derived from the peaceful uses of his explosives, yet the terrible use to which they were to be put during the war has left a vague impression in the public mind that he was himself an arms king and that the awards were the result of a guilty conscience. This is no more than a half-truth. Born in Stockholm in 1833 and brought up in St. Petersburg, where his father had a small armaments engineering business, he was a sickly, introspective youth who suffered from a variety of ailments, including convulsions, migraine, neurasthenia and angina. An unusually intelligent boy who was privately tutored up to the age of 16, he knew five languages and was deeply attracted to literature.

It was his father who first interested him in nitroglycerin, and at the age of 30 Alfred had the shattering experience of seeing his brother Emil and four others killed in a laboratory explosion of a nitroglycerin mixture. Three years later, in 1867, he had incorporated the unstable substance with kieselguhr, an absorptive mineral; he called the result dynamite, from a Greek word meaning "power." He was a brilliant businessman as well as a brilliant chemist and for this, as for all his inventions, he took out patents all over the world. In the next eight years his experiments with guncotton and nitroglycerin produced blasting gelatin; and 13 years later, in 1888, only eight years before his death, he produced ballistite.

His life was explosive in every sense of the word. Experimenting as he was with highly dangerous materials and constructing factories throughout the world for their manufacture, he was bound to encounter accidents. In 1866, 70 cases of nitroglycerin shipped from Nobel's factory in Germany blew up a freighter in a Panamanian port, killing or injuring 50 people. The New Jersey works of the Blasting Oil Company, his first venture in the United States, blew up a few years later. This company had held his American patents, and its president, Taliaferro Preston Shaffner, an unscrupulous promoter who had become his business associate in the early days, was responsible for much of the hateful publicity Nobel received in the United States, which, one suspects, considerably strengthened his misanthropic tendencies. Paul Barbe, who looked after his French affairs, turned out little better. The endless litigation which followed induced him to write: "We are dealing with a pack of crooked lawyers and bloodsuckers." In the same letter he added: "Nothing is more dangerous than to be a director of a French stock company." In Britain Nobel found that his brains had been picked and a variation of ballistite patented as cordite.

IN 1892 he hired a personal adviser on peace. By then he was already considering ways and means of encouraging disarmament, envisaging a world tribunal for the settlement of differences between nations. He became obsessed by the idea of peace and entered into long discussions with Bertha von Suttner, who in 1889 had published a controversial novel called *Lay Down Your Arms* and was organizing a popular peace movement. It was to her that he is supposed to have confided that he wished he could invent a substance or machine so frightful that wars would become impossible. The result of all this—his loneliness, his frailties, his life dedicated to explosives, the shady characters that had formed the background to so much of his business world—was the will of 1895. One wonders what this strange man would have thought of the worldwide prestige of the awards he willed, what he would have thought of the United Nations, which is in a sense a projection of the ideas he formulated before either of the two great wars that were its birth pains had been fought.

Although the name Nobel was important in the projection of Scandinavia's peaceful image, it was Fridtjof Nansen, an explorer turned diplomat and humanitarian, who laid the foundations of that image. Two more dissimilar men than Nansen and Nobel can scarcely be imagined. Nansen was tough physically, his world the icecaps of Greenland and the polar seas. He was born near Oslo in 1861, and in the almost 70 years of his life—he did not die until 1930—he revived the old Viking tradition of exploration among Norwegians, assisted at the birth of his country's independence and devoted his later years to relieving some of the chaos and wretchedness left by World War I. His personality, his consideration for others and, above all, his great capacity for leadership made him a sort of father figure to the new state he had helped to create; in 1922 he was awarded the Nobel Peace Prize.

T HERE was no indication at the outset of Nansen's career of the role he was to play later. After graduating from Oslo University with a degree in zoology, Nansen made a voyage in the Greenland sea in the sealer *Viking*. He was then 21 and the trip, which gave him his first glimpse of the Greenland icecap, made a deep impression. Greenland had never been crossed, and on his return Nansen began to plan. He was already an expert skier and his plans were based on the use of skis and his experience of winter life in the mountains of north Norway. As curator of zoology in the Bergen museum, a post to which he was appointed in 1882, he had access to a great deal of information and he had studied the methods of Norway's arctic hunters. In 1888 he was ready for his first big venture, which involved a landing on the uninhabited east coast of Greenland and a direct ski crossing of the unknown interior with no base to fall back on. The only hope of survival was to reach the settlements on the opposite coast. He did, in 75 days.

Nansen's next venture was even more ambitious, nothing less than an entirely revolutionary attempt on the North Pole, at that time an apparently unattainable goal. Otto Sverdrup had been one of the party of five that had crossed Greenland with him. They had noted that logs from Siberia and Alaska had drifted to the west Greenland shores; they had also identified driftwood from the American ship *Jeannette*, wrecked off the New Siberian Islands on the opposite side of the Arctic. Their plan was to build a ship that could withstand the colossal pressures of the ice pack, sail it into the ice and let the polar currents do the rest.

T HE ship was the *Fram*, today open to inspection in a museum shed in Oslo, complete with all equipment and life-sized figures dressed in the actual clothing worn on various expeditions. The colossal size and the intricate placing of the innumerable great bow timbers gives some idea of the accurate understanding Nansen and his shipbuilders held of the lateral thrust of the arctic ice.

Nansen's conviction that the East Greenland Current was a continuation of a northwest current running from the Bering Straits proved correct. *Fram*, with Otto Sverdrup as captain, was sailed into the ice pack in the neighborhood of the New Siberian Islands in 1893. In her three-year drift she reached latitude 85° 55' N. In March 1895, Nansen, with Hjalmar Johansen as sole companion, left the ship and traveling by dog sled reached 86° 14' N., the highest latitude attained to that date. They wintered in Franz Josef Land and were picked up by a British expedition, returning to Norway at the same time that the *Fram* emerged at Spitsbergen. A highly original piece of exploration, the drift of the *Fram* was a brilliant success, bringing Nansen world fame. Scientifically it was of the greatest importance and his writings on the subject established him as the leader in the new science of oceanography.

Other explorers were now mounting scientific expeditions and this peaceful penetration of unexplored areas of the globe was in marked contrast to the maneuverings of the great powers in the years immediately preceding World War I. In fact, it was these expeditions that established Norway in the world's mind as a country determined to express its toughness by peaceful rather than warlike means. From 1898 to 1902 Sverdrup explored the islands to the west of north Greenland, the ski and dog-sled technique originated by Nansen being used extensively for discovery and scientific research. And then another Norwegian explorer, Roald Amundsen, made his debut.

In 1905 Amundsen became the first man ever to take a ship through the Northwest Passage. During his three-year trip, he made a number of observations of the properties of the Magnetic North Pole, and probably actually crossed over it. Then he planned and successfully carried out a ski and dog-sled attack on the South Pole. He arrived there in December 1911, just a month before a British expedition led by Captain Robert Scott, who perished with his entire party on the return trip.

THE tragedy of the Scott expedition has to some extent overshadowed the Norwegian achievement; gallant failure is often more captivating to the public imagination than success. Nevertheless, Amundsen's victory was a dramatic demonstration of superior technique and sound planning. His plan for another drift through the arctic seas was delayed by World War I, but in 1918 Amundsen was able to take a new vessel, the *Maud*, on an expedition to the Arctic.

Amundsen himself eventually left the ship to make an airplane flight across the Pole but had to abandon the attempt when the plane's skis collapsed on take-off. He was nevertheless the first explorer to appreciate the future of planes in the Arctic. Later he made two airborne expeditions, the first in 1925 with two planes, the second a year later by dirigible. Little more than a quarter of a century later the Scandinavian Airlines System inaugurated the first regular flights to the United States across the North Pole.

But Amundsen and all the lesser Norwegian explorers—Thor Heyerdahl, for example, who with other scientists successfully completed a 101-day drift in a balsa raft across the Pacific in 1947 in an effort to corroborate a theory that Polynesia was originally settled by emigrants from South America—have done no more than maintain the tradition of exploration established by Nansen. None of their expeditions has achieved as much scientifically as that first three-year drift of *Fram;* nor as men do they match him in stature.

AS a diplomat, Nansen headed the delegation which asked Prince Carl of Denmark (later Haakon VII) to become Norway's king after the country became independent of Sweden in 1905. His success in this resulted in his being appointed the first Norwegian minister to England. After World War I, it was Nansen who led and inspired the Norwegians to work for international peace through the League of Nations, devoting much of his time and energy first to the problem of repatriation of prisoners of war and later to famine relief in Russia and the plight of some 1.3 million Russian and Armenian refugees. During this period, he developed the "Nansen passport," an identity card for displaced persons which was internationally accepted.

It was against this background, and the recollection of Norway's gallant stand in World War II, that Trygve Lie was invited to become the United Nations' first Secretary-General. A Swede would not have been acceptable at that time; Swedish neutrality during the war had a tarnished look to countries only just emerged from a life-and-death struggle. Eight years later, the situation was different. The North Atlantic Treaty Organization had been established as a counterbalance to the Soviet bloc. Norway and Denmark had abandoned neutrality and joined with the West. Sweden, alone among the Scandinavian countries, remained entirely neutral, and thus acceptable to both East and West. And there was the memory of the services rendered to the U.N. and international peace by Sweden's Count Folke Bernadotte.

The Bernadottes are descended from Jean Baptiste Bernadotte, a son of a French lawyer. He joined Napoleon's army as a sergeant, rose to be one of its foremost marshals and in 1810 was offered the Swedish crown. His descendant was Count Folke Bernadotte. Born in 1895, Bernadotte served in the army, but his interests were humanitarian, centering first on the Boy Scout movement and then the Swedish Red Cross. He emerged as an international figure during World War II when as a Red Cross official he arranged the exchange of prisoners of war. In 1945 he negotiated the liberation of some 19,000 Norwegians and Danes from German concentration camps. Shortly afterward he leaped into the news as the recipient of the last-minute offer by Heinrich Himmler, Hitler's Gestapo chief, to surrender to the West in an effort to prevent the imminent Russian invasion of Germany.

In dealing with one of the United Nations' first major problems after the war, the Security Council gave Bernadotte the task of mediating between the Jews and the Arabs in Palestine. It was while he was attempting to carry out this almost impossible job that he was assassinated on September 17, 1948.

HIS death was a great loss to Sweden and to the world. He was a very able negotiator, dedicated to the service of international peace. Had he lived he might well have become Secretary-General of the United Nations, for he had all the necessary qualities. Instead, when the nations turned to Sweden, it was on Dag Hammarskjöld that the choice fell. Hammarskjöld was an economist who came into international politics after serving as chairman of his country's National Bank and in the foreign ministry. His strength was essentially that of a theoretician, a man of brilliant, lucid, detached mind; his weakness, an obstinate determination to mold events to a preconceived pattern.

As Trygve Lie said when he was Secretary-General: "The U.N. has to do the world's most impossible task." With the sole exception of Denmark, the Scandinavian countries possessed virtually no experience of colonial responsibility, and this was almost certainly a handicap when, during the last years of his Secretary-Generalship, Hammarskjöld became involved in first Arab, and then African nationalism. These were problems requiring an entirely different approach from that demanded by the previous cold war maneuvers of East and West which had theretofore been the main preoccupation of the U.N. Secretariat. For his handling of the Congo, Hammarskjöld drew bitter criticism from those who felt that he regarded all administrators and officials of colonial countries as suspect and that he denied the territory the administrative experience it so desperately needed to fill the vacuum left by the Belgians. While the employment of only "neutral" forces and leaders may have been sound in theory, the practice undoubtedly contributed to the conditions of suspicion and chaos which prevailed in the Congo.

WHATEVER the mistakes, the U.N. owes much to Scandinavia. For a decade and a half, through Korea, Berlin, Suez and the Congo, through the Arab-Israeli conflict and all the lesser crises, through the growth of voting power within the Assembly of new nations whose views often lacked a basis of responsibility, Lie and Hammarskjöld set the stamp of their personalities upon international events. The characters of both men were typical of their own countries, and both drew strength from the lands of their birth. It was characteristic of the Norwegian Trygve Lie that on relinquishing the Secretary-Generalship he should retire to the bleak Røros plateau of central Norway to write his book *In the Cause of Peace*. He concluded that book with these words: "Were it only possible for the rest of humanity to share this simple peace and freedom of the Norwegian mountains, how much happier the world's millions would be!" This he felt deeply —the peace of the mountains, of lake and open sea. In them the Scandinavians find their sense of freedom, their love of peace.

Dag Hammarskjöld, later killed in a plane crash, stands in an office at the United Nations, an organization he helped strengthen.

Selfless Searchers for World Harmony

Among the leading men of modern Scandinavia have been peacemakers like Trygve Lie and Dag Hammarskjöld. Even more remarkable have been the scientists—Alfred Nobel, Fridtjof Nansen, Niels Bohr—who were also men of peace. Devoted to exploring their chosen fields, they have been equally concerned with helping find paths to world harmony and order. With a detachment born of the clear northern mind, they have been devoted servants of all mankind.

*FRIDTJOF NANSEN, who
achieved fame as a daring explorer,
later turned his energies
to working for humanitarian causes*

Nansen's specially built ship "Fram" is locked in the ice in Janu

Engulfed by a mob of Armenians, Nansen personally distributes s

YOUNG HERO of Arctic exploration, Nansen poses (*left*) after his return to Norway from the *Fram* expedition. He was a leading oceanographer as well as explorer.

395 on its three-year drifting journey through the polar ice cap.

INTERNATIONAL FIGURE, Nansen *(above, left)* takes part in ceremonies which proclaimed him an honorary rector in St. Andrews University in Scotland in 1926.

the food he collected for the relief of that region after World War I.

AGING STATESMAN at the League of Nations, Nansen *(far right)* confers with Britain's Lord Robert Cecil, who like Nansen was a winner of the Nobel Peace Prize.

NIELS BOHR helped formulate atomic theory and then worked for the control of nuclear weapons

YOUNG PHYSICIST and Nobel Prize winner (1922) for his bold insights into atomic structure, Bohr *(above, right)* meets with Nansen *(pages 108-109).*

ERUDITE TEACHER at his own world-leading Institute for Theoretical Physics in Copenhagen, Niels Bohr lectures earnestly to visiting scientists.

"MANSION OF HONOR" given Bohr for life as Denmark's leading scientist forms the backdrop for this portrait of the physicist and his wife.

SERIOUS DISCUSSION engages Bohr and a colleague in the laboratory of the Institute. Mourning was worldwide when Bohr died in late 1962.

Timber, Snow and Sea

FOREST and water, mountain, lake and river in flood, the cold dark of winter, the milk-white nights of summer all too short, and always the eternal snows, the glaciers lying heavy on the heights to peer over rims of primeval rock. This is the northland—the upper edge of the Scandinavia that swings more than a thousand miles southward out of the frigid Barents Sea. Where snow and glaciers melt away, the tree line starts, and below the trees, the lakes, the fjords and the rivers tumble to the sea. To see all this a man must leave his car and use his legs, walking and climbing in summer with a rucksack on his back, trekking the

forest ways on skis when the trees are all winter-white; in any season taking to the boats that ply the fjords and the inner leads between the islands. Then, and then only, he becomes a part of the hard northland and can understand how the Norsemen live, how a man like Jan Baalsrud, sole survivor of a commando landing in northern Norway in 1943, could lie badly injured on a mountaintop through a blizzard and survive more than six weeks in a hell of bitter cold, hacking his frostbitten toes from his feet with a penknife.

Such tales bring the northland to life, but it is still difficult for men of milder climates to understand why the people of Finnmark in the north of Norway went back after World War II. They had been evacuated south after every town, settlement and farmstead had been ruthlessly destroyed in the German retreat in 1945. They had seen the softer life of the lowlands and had been offered work and land for resettlement. Yet they insisted on returning to face the cold and the bitter task of rebuilding all that had been lost. Why? What was it that sent them north again?

A TRAVELER in the northland knows the answer. To the people of the north, the north is beautiful, the hardness of the life a source of satisfaction, of contentment and happiness. It is the same with men born to sea and forest. For 10,000 years man has lived up here in the cold silence of forest and water. The trees gave him timber for his homestead, and wood for his skis and his boats; there he found forest animals who supplied fur and meat. In the water was an abundance of food.

Money as the medium of exchange came slowly to this part of the world. But though island and forest homesteads were always virtually self-sufficient, breeding an independent, virile race, the idea of barter was established on the coast the moment man stitched hides to bent timbers and was able to use the water as a means of transporting himself and his produce from place to place.

With this background in mind, it can be seen that the evolution of man to his present circumstances in this northland has been an inevitable process, little affected by external events. Nevertheless, it is upon the wealth and requirements of the rest of the world that the relative prosperity of modern Scandinavia has been built. The forests of Sweden and Norway would never have given birth to the huge timber industry of today without world demand. It was the incredible growth in the world's consumption of pulp and packaging materials around the end of the 19th Century that supplied the original impetus. At first the industry was relatively small, existing chiefly for local demand —timber for houses, for farm buildings and farm work, for fires, for furniture and ships.

In both Sweden and Norway the visitor is very conscious of being in a land of trees, particularly when driving through the hill and lake country to the south and east of the great central spine of the Scandinavian mountains. Here forests of spruce and pine clothe the landscape, and where it is too cold for conifers, the ubiquitous birch, queen of the Arctic, takes over, all silvered daintiness shivering in the wind. On the long lakes, scoured north and south by the melted glaciers of past ice ages, great choked masses of logs add their pattern to the scene, waiting to be consumed by the inevitable sawmill or pulp plant, or held in readiness for the next spring rush of the melted snows which will carry them down the rivers to the sea. And along the southern coasts small tugs steam through the inner leads, towing behind them thousands of logs steel-banded into rafts like half-submerged barges, taking them to the industrial plants that seem to lurk in every inlet. The mills send up plumes of white smoke as they convert the cut trees into pulp, paper, cardboard and cellulose, into lumber, furniture, even matches, all the products that the modern world expects from the softwood forests of the north.

THE forest that had given birth to the long ships of the Viking Age brought prosperity to Norway as far back as the 16th and 17th Centuries. Because of this the Norwegians have been conscious for a long time of the need to cultivate natural regeneration. Good forestry is not just a matter of clear felling and waiting for nature to replenish the store. Nature needs help to repair the ravages of man. Norway today is cutting around 275 million cubic feet a year, which is about three quarters of the annual growth. With modern methods of reforestation, the reclamation of swamps and extensive planting, the country reckons on increasing its annual timber output by as much as 50 per cent. Sweden, which is cutting more than 1.7 billion cubic feet annually, is also striving for an increase in forestry production, for both countries must still import from Finland to feed their timber processing plants.

Denmark lost its forests very early in its history. It seems incredible now, when almost the length and breadth of this small country can be traveled without sight of anything that could be called a forest stand, to realize that Jutland and all the neighboring islands were covered as late as the 10th Century by as dense a tree growth as were the more northern countries. Centuries of unrestricted felling to make way for small farms destroyed much of this priceless legacy. By the end of the 18th Century only about 4 per cent of the land was still covered by forest growth.

THREATENED by a shortage of timber for houses and ships, even for firewood, the Danish government passed legislation in 1805 that is the basis of the highly efficient Danish forestry system to this day. Since then, the forested land area has increased to 10 per cent, with an annual output of about 71 million cubic feet. This is small by comparison with the yield in Norway and Sweden, but it nevertheless represents a considerable achievement.

The prosperity of Scandinavia is as closely linked to its other natural asset, water, as it is to the forests. Many areas of the world have coastlines that give a seafaring tradition to their people, but there are few areas that have a longer coastline in proportion to land areas. In Norway, in addition, the off-lying rocks and islands provide an almost uninterrupted inner lead through which sea transport can proceed sheltered from storms. These islands and the deep indentations of the fjords also offer innumerable havens. Moreover, the inland sea of the Baltic, although treacherous because of currents that vary with wind direction and unpleasant seas which get up very quickly in a blow, makes the movement of cargoes among the three countries themselves, and to Germany, Russia and Finland, a relatively simple matter.

All these favorable factors gave impetus to the mercantile and colonialist expansion of the

Viking Age. The Hansa merchants of North Germany and the Dutch also later made good use of them. But though Viking power suffered an eclipse in the Middle Ages, the seafaring tradition that had helped bring it into being continued uninterrupted, particularly in Norway and Denmark, where fishing has long been an important basic industry.

It remains so today. In the Lofoten Islands, three quarters of the way up the coast of Norway and well inside the Arctic Circle, some 1,500 boats manned by about 12,000 men gather in the harbors each spring for the cod fishing. It is one of the greatest concentrations of fishermen in the world, and in the islands they serve fresh-caught cod as a delicacy greater than salmon. Northward, all along the coast of Finnmark, the smell of fish oil hangs over the quays, and on the rocks behind the little wooden settlements great racks stand packed with fish hung in the cold air to dry. Winter herring, mackerel, coalfish, haddock, halibut—the size of Norway's catch varies from year to year, but it is always considerably more than a million tons and in the peak year of 1956 it reached 2.2 million tons.

IN Denmark the same fish oil smell hangs reeking over ports like Thyborøn at the entrance to Lim Fjord. Here and at Esbjerg and other North Sea ports the trawling fleets lie close-packed, a dark array of masts and nets hung drying against the broad skies of a country almost as flat as Holland. Denmark's is not nearly such a big industry as Norway's, for the Danes chiefly fish the North Sea banks, which are suffering now from indiscriminate trawling, and there is not the same marvelous replenishment in that area that the Gulf Stream brings to the northern waters. Nevertheless, Denmark still has some 12,500 boats and 17,000 men who bring in a yearly catch of more than half a million tons. The Greenland and Faeroe Island fishermen net an additional 150,000 tons. Even in Sweden, where the fisheries are not important in relation to industry as a whole, there are about 10,000 men involved, although their catch each year averages only about 250,000 tons.

In every little port in the Baltic, and there are many of them, fish is bought at the quay, and the buyer selects just what he wants from fish traps where his food is swimming live. Nobody· in these countries would dream of eating stale frozen fish. Here eel is regarded as a delicacy, as it is in Holland, and a man can earn almost $5,000 in a short three-month season, working his eel nets with two small boats in the shallow inland seas.

Throughout Scandinavia fish is more than a staple food; it is almost a way of life. And the greatest fish of all is the herring. No fish can be served in so many different ways, and in Norway it is as likely to appear on the breakfast table as at *aftens*, the evening meal. *Røget sild* and titbits are only two of the innumerable different forms in which herring appears, particularly in Denmark. In Sweden, for the connoisseur, there is *surströmming*, raw herring that has been allowed to ferment for a year. In the cooking of fish the Swedes use the herb dill a great deal. The Norwegians cook trout in sour cream and serve their salmon with horse-radish sauce. Norwegian salmon is the finest in the world and *gravlaks*—raw salmon that has been subjected to pressure for a few days after being salted and spiced—is often more delicious than even smoked salmon. And in season, to conclude each meal, are the fruits of heath and forest—the *multebaer*, or cloudberry, and the wood strawberry that grows in profusion in the south of Norway and Sweden.

The whale, which since Viking days has been caught off the coasts of north Norway, has always provided food as well as oil. Whale meat was in great demand in Scandinavia during the

period of severe rationing that followed World War II and it fetched high prices, a 60- to 70-ton carcass bringing between $1,000 and $3,000 for the meat alone, and about $3,000 for the oil extracted from the blubber.

The story of modern whaling is essentially Norwegian. The great American and British whaling fleets of the 19th Century vanished with the advent of steam and the impetus given to trade by the industrial revolution. Cargo-carrying became more profitable than whaling, already hit by the switch to mineral rather than whale oil for lighting. There were additional factors as well. A series of disasters in the Arctic had depleted the sailing fleets, and northern waters, overhunted for years, gradually had become less productive. Whaling was ready to shift to the Antarctic, where the huge blue whale and the fin whale were known to exist in great numbers. And when it did, Norwegian whalers were prepared to go south with it.

As early as the 1860s Svend Foyn, a Norwegian seal hunter, had invented the grenade harpoon. Fired from a gun, it had an explosive warhead designed to burst inside the whale and kill it outright. By the turn of the century boats fast enough to cope with the speedy blue and fin whales had become available, and in 1904 Carl A. Larsen, who had already led three Norwegian expeditions south to the Antarctic to reconnoiter, commenced whaling operations from a shore station on South Georgia, which lies on the edge of the Antarctic pack ice. The following year Christen Christensen sent a floating factory ship of sorts to operate in the Antarctic, and for the next 20 years ever larger factory ships supplemented the shore stations.

WHY WHALES ARE VALUABLE

The whaling fleets of Norway and other nations have declined in size over the past century, but the whale remains a much sought-after animal. Although whale oil has not been used for lighting or heating since the 1880s, it remains employed in the manufacture of such diverse products as soap, fertilizer, crayons, lipstick, polishes, detergent alcohol and dynamite. In addition, the whale pituitary supplies extracts for the production of artificial hormones, and the throat yields materials utilized in the treatment of thyroid conditions. Some substances, such as ambergris, a fatty secretion employed as a base for fine perfumes, are obtainable only from the whale.

The fact that the crews had to flense the whales, stripping the blubber from them as they floated alongside the ships, called for calm weather or a sheltered anchorage. It was a limiting factor which was not surmounted until 1925, when the *Lancing*, the first open-ended factory ship which could haul the whales on board through a slipway in its stern, sailed from Norway for the Antarctic. It was able to operate for the whole season independent of any shore base. This was the prototype of the modern ocean expedition, and the death sentence for thousands upon thousands of whales.

WHALING has been a strange and very profitable industry. At its peak in the 1950s there were annually some 20 separate Antarctic expeditions involved—Dutch, Russian, Japanese and British, as well as Norwegian. They used a total of more than 200 ships, including catchers, tow boats, refrigerated vessels and tankers. Planes were used as spotters and the factory ships themselves were as big as liners, up to 26,000 tons. Half the expeditions were from Norwegian ports, and the British ships employed a high percentage of Norwegians.

Now, however, the bloody harvest—and it is a bloody one, which would not be tolerated for a moment on land, for the harpoon rarely kills instantly and a mortally wounded whale will drag a 300-ton ship for miles—is but a shadow of its former self. Seventeen nations adhered to an international convention in 1946 which limited the total catch but set no quotas for the individual nations. Fierce competition resulted, and new factory ships and other equipment were introduced. Faced with rising operating costs and a decline in the price of whale oil, the industry is not the profitable one it was.

Fishing and whaling have provided the cornerstones on which the Scandinavians have built up two other vital sea-born industries: shipping and shipbuilding. Every country's mercantile strength was originally founded on fishing communities, the days of sail particularly requiring hereditary skill and a natural aptitude for the sea. Norwegian fishermen had the advantage of

Gulf Stream spawning grounds protected by rocks and islands. Small boats thus could always fish in shelter.

Even now, although the Norwegians took to deep-sea trawling some 40 years ago, Norway's shores are thick with more than 40,000 fishing boats, including small *toc-a-tocs* operating from local settlements. This has gone on for centuries. It was the fishing industry that brought the Hansa merchants to Bergen, and when the Dutch moved in to capture the timber trade, the Norwegians began to realize the possibilities of the carrying trade. With a background of centuries of cargo-carrying between settlements and across the open-sea stretches at the mouths of the big fjords, their merchant fleet developed rapidly, helped by the growth of world trade.

By the beginning of the 20th Century their merchant fleet was important enough for the Norwegians to demand that Sweden, which controlled Norway at the time, grant them a separate consular service; it was partly this demand that led to Norway's break to independence in 1905. By the beginning of World War II the Norwegian fleet was the most modern in the world; in size it ranked fourth with a total of almost five million tons.

MOST of this tonnage was on the high seas when the Germans invaded in 1940. This large fleet served the Allied cause. By the end of the war almost two and a half million tons had been sunk. The speed and determination with which Norway thereupon replaced its merchant tonnage is one of the most astonishing achievements of the postwar era. Careful, as are all people who live in a hard climate, the Norwegians plowed back money without regard to the hardships they had to face under stringent rationing, currency restrictions and high taxation. Within four years Norway had more than replaced its wartime losses, and now its fleet totals 12 million tons, half of it tankers.

The Danes, who built up a Baltic fleet in the wake of the Dutch and whose navy was a powerful force when Norway was only beginning to establish its mercantile strength, now possess slightly more than two million tons of shipping, 60 per cent of it from Denmark's own yards. Sweden's fleet is bigger—about four million tons; oddly enough, however, Sweden's own ships, many of them specialized carriers, are largely concerned with other nations' products, while more than half of Sweden's own trade is carried by foreign vessels. Sweden is, in fact, more interested in building ships than in sailing them; its shipbuilding industry is the fourth largest in the world.

Scandinavia's shipping interests, it is clear, are extraordinarily large in relation to the number of people—more than a ton of shipping per person, and more if you include the multitude of small boats. But figures do not give any idea of the impact made on the visitor who takes the trouble to explore the coasts. It is not difficult. With relatively few exceptions, and those mainly in Sweden, the chief towns, even the capital cities, are ports. Ferries are everywhere as common as buses in other countries, and ships run scheduled trips to all the main islands, plying the waterways of the inner leads from the Gulf of Bothnia through the Skagerrak and all the way up the long west coast of Norway.

FEW persons visiting Stockholm bother to take a trip through the Skärgård, that lovely litter of 7,000 rocky islands and islets guarding the entrance to Sweden's capital. The wild beauty of Denmark's Lim Fjord, with its broad inlets and narrow, dredged channels marked by brooms, is almost unknown to outsiders; so, too, are the minute harbors, like Nyord Havn with an entrance only 25 feet wide on the shallow inland sea of the Bøgestrøm, and the doll's house villages scattered like toys along inland waterways such as Årøsund and Smålands Farvandet. Even the old ship ports of Svendborg, Sønderborg, Fåborg and Falsterbo are hardly known, lying off the beaten track.

The visitor to Oslo is seldom aware of the beauty of the 60-mile fjord that is the sea approach to Norway's capital, or of the maze of islands reached by narrow waterways that lie at its entrance, guarding the fjord approach to the whaling ports of Tønsberg and Sandefjord. Fredrikstad is typical, a riverway flowing through a white wood town with the rust-blotched hulks of great ships in for repairs almost blocking the passage. Along Sweden's west-facing coast are deep inlets leading to the great shipbuilding centers, the coast littered with bare, bald rocks where nothing grows, as though the ice that long ago scourged them clean of vegetation had only just receded. But at Single Fjord, which is the boundary between Sweden and Norway, the black granite heaps are suddenly clothed with trees and the land is green.

AND all down the south Norway coast an intricate lacing of seaways winds through rock and tree growth, marvelously signposted with buoys painted red and black and big granite beacons. In the narrower channels, some only a few yards wide, iron poles are set on the rocks with an arm to indicate which side to pass.

At the Naze, the most southerly tip of Norway, it is different. Now the coast faces the North Sea—the Atlantic. The offshore islands guarding the coast are gone, the navigational marks few. Even north of Stavanger, where the great Inner Lead that is used by the ships taking tourists to the midnight sun begins, pilotage is difficult; in fact, to qualify as a pilot a man must spend a year plying this route unpaid to learn by eye and experience more than 2,000 transit marks. And through that Inner Lead, the old Viking route, three ports a day is not too much, so close-packed are the wooden fishing settlements, each with its cannery or fish processing plant, its inshore boats and the still, cold light that has the translucent quality of the far north. Who can ever forget the sight of the sun at midnight, throwing the jagged, serrated outline of the Lofoten Islands into black relief, the black ice of the Svartisen Glacier south of Bodø lying cold and wicked on the coastline rocks, or the varnished wood of the fishing fleet putting to sea in thick mist from the most northerly port on Magerøy? All this, which is both beautiful and strange to see, is the natural background to life in the north.

A crewman stands bundled against a freezing wind aboard a fishing boat as it plows through a rough sea off the Lofoten Islands.

The Rigorous Life of Arctic Fishermen

Among Scandinavia's best fishing grounds are the waters near the Lofoten Islands, a string of rocky humps off Norway's west coast. From the islands' tiny ports hundreds of small craft go out during the late winter fishing season to battle storms and bring home a catch of codfish. As shown in these pictures by Howard Sochurek, the work is hard and the islands isolated, but still the men fish and their sons yearn for the day when they too will become mariners.

WEATHERED PILOTHOUSE of the Lofoten Island fishing boat *Midnatsol* (Midnight Sun) is crusted with driven snow after enduring long, cold hours in the open ocean.

CHEERFUL CREW gathers at lunchtime in the *Midnatsol's* cabin to eat simple sandwiches of bread and cheese or jam and to warm their fingers around mugs of hot coffee.

EXPERIENCED DECK HAND hauls cod over the gunwale of the *Midnatsol (left)* which normally trawls with many long lines carrying a total of about 4,000 baited hooks.

A SMALL WHALE is pulled aboard another Lofoten Island boat, the *Northwind*, which is armed with a harpoon gun. This four-ton whale produced 5,280 pounds of meat and some valuable oil, but whale fishing is financially risky since whales are now rare in the arctic seas and a boat may go for days without sighting a catch.

BATCH OF COD is carried on a yoke to drying racks at the port of Henningsvaer. Most of the catch is decapitated, cleaned and hung to dry in the arctic winds.

CROWD OF BOATS nearly fills the tiny harbor of Henningsvaer *(right)*, a town of only 1,500 people which sometimes shelters 800 boats during the fishing season.

FISHERMAN'S BOY, aged 11, works after school cutting bait, fixing it on hooks and storing the baited lines in barrels. A boy can make $50 baiting during the winter.

CREW'S TASK after reaching port is to cut off the cod heads and ready the fish for the drying racks. The heads are also dried and then ground up for fertilizer.

CONFIRMATION in the village Lutheran church is a traditional rite for Lofoten Island boys, who are then allowed to leave school and go to sea with their fathers.

CONVERSATION at society meetings breaks the tedium for the island women of Vaerøy. Among their good works is a fund to give island wives mainland vacations.

CONGRATULATIONS are offered a newly confirmed boy, Lennarth Andreassen of Vaerøy *(center, above)*, by family and neighbors at a large cake and coffee party. His mother serves, dressed in the costume of her native region. Elaborate pastries, including a traditional Norwegian *bløtkake*, have been in preparation for days.

9

Culture in a Cold Climate

ONE of the most surprising features of the Scandinavian peoples is their cultural enthusiasm—surprising because in winter as well as summer they have unrivaled outlets for physical recreation. Take books, for instance. While figures are difficult to obtain, it has been estimated that yearly sales in Sweden amount to some 23 million and in Denmark and Norway to about eight million each, a total of about 40 million for the three countries.

In addition, all the Scandinavian countries have flourishing public libraries. Sweden, for example, has 4,462 libraries with a stock of 27 million books. More than two million people use these libraries, borrowing some 48 million volumes a year. Danish library borrowings of about 28 million are still higher in proportion to the population, and even Norway, with its scattered communities, records yearly borrowings of more than six million. The Scandinavians are just about the most voracious readers in the world.

There are two basic reasons for this high level of reading. One is compulsory education, which produced general literacy much earlier in the Scandinavian nations than in most other countries; the other is the spare time afforded by long, dark winter nights. An example of the effect of the latter is the rapid growth of the Norwegian publishing house of Mortensen. Early this century Ernst G. Mortensen started a correspondence school in Oslo to meet the frustrated desire for knowledge among adults in the isolated settlements of the north. The result far exceeded his expectations. Norwegians in the thousands applied for his courses, which now cover almost every conceivable subject. The inevitable development of this was learning through entertainment—in other words, magazines. Now Mortensen publishes the most widely circulated magazines in Norway, and the 180-odd correspondence courses, although still in great demand, are but a small part of the company's business.

THIS high level of literacy encouraged standards of writing quite exceptional for countries with such small populations, and it was the most sparsely populated of these countries, Norway, that produced the writer of the greatest stature. Henrik Ibsen was born at Skien in 1828. He was apprenticed to an apothecary at Grimstad at the age of 16, eight years after his father's speculations had brought the family to ruin. This was the background against which he began to write, producing his first drama, *Catiline*, at the age of 21. But it was not until he went to live in Oslo that he really began to come to grips with his subjects. The abandonment of Denmark by Norway and Sweden to the German invaders in the war of 1864 so incensed him that he exiled himself from his homeland for the next 10 years, producing two great poetic dramas—*Brand*, and the more widely known *Peer Gynt*.

When Ibsen was over 50, he began to publish the series of noteworthy plays that has since been revived all over the world—*A Doll's House* (1879), *Ghosts* (1881), *An Enemy of the People* (1882), *The Wild Duck* (1884), *Rosmersholm* (1886), *Hedda Gabler* (1890) and *The Master Builder* (1892). No other Scandinavian writer has his international reputation; indeed, there are few playwrights in the world who rank as his equal. With poetic sensitivity and brilliant technical control, he examined public and private morality, relations between men and women, and the struggle between individual and society. It is difficult to realize what a storm Ibsen raised at the time. His violent and emotional comment on the social world of his day was something new in the theater. On Ibsen's 70th birthday, George Bernard Shaw wrote characteristically that his impact on England was "almost equal to the influence which three revolutions, six crusades, a couple of foreign invasions and an earthquake would produce."

Ibsen was influenced by that other great Norwegian writer, Bjørnstjerne Bjørnson, who was his contemporary, and both were influenced by their predecessor, the poet Henrik Wergeland. It was a great period of Norwegian letters, a sort of golden age encouraged by a political climate tending toward liberalism. Bjørnson was essentially a political writer, agitator as well as poet and playwright, and his work, like that of Wergeland and Wergeland's sister, the novelist Camilla Collett, is little known internationally. Better known is Knut Hamsun, a brilliant Norwegian novelist who wrote *Hunger*, a study of a writer starving to death, and *Growth of the Soil*, an epic of a farmer's struggle against nature and society. Hamsun won the Nobel Prize in 1920 but died despised by most of his countrymen for his outspoken pro-Nazi views in World War II.

IN Sweden, Johan August Strindberg, 20 years Ibsen's junior, was also building an international reputation. A strange, warped personality, plagued by fits of depression, he nevertheless produced a great volume of important work. For a time he devoted his energies to the study of chemistry. He experimented on his own brain and body. Politically he supported the growing labor movement, but his interests ranged through mysticism and alchemy to journalism. He was a misogynist who married three women. The best known of all the prolific outpourings of his genius are *The Father*, in which a strong man is driven mad by his scheming, supposedly weaker wife, and

Miss Julie, in which an aristocratic young woman is irresistibly and disastrously drawn to a servant in her father's house. A writer whose later works are permeated by the theme "man is to be pitied," Strindberg has had a lasting effect on dramatic form and expression.

IN complete contrast to Strindberg was the much-loved Swedish author Selma Lagerlöf, who was born at a country estate called Mårbacka in 1858. She was the first woman to receive the Nobel Prize for literature and the first to be elected to the Swedish Academy. Coming from a Värmland country family, she had an urgent desire to write a great novel of the Swedish farmer. She did this in *The Tale of a Manor*, which, next to *The Story of Gösta Berling*, her first book, is the most widely read of her novels. But in the international field she is probably best known for her "Goose Boy" stories, the adventures of a small boy who flies north to Lappland and later to foreign lands on the back of a wild goose. *The Wonderful Adventures of Nils* was first published in 1906-1907. Translations followed, and even a Russian film. With the proceeds, Selma Lagerlöf bought back the family home of Mårbacka—from which many of the scenes and characters in her novels had been fondly drawn—and in her old age she became something of a legend. She died in 1940, aged 82.

Denmark, too, had its great literary figure— Hans Christian Andersen. For a time his international reputation was greater than that of any other Scandinavian writer. His fairy tales have been known to children of all countries for more than a century now, yet few know his strange story, his desperate early struggles. He was born in 1805, somewhat earlier than the other great Nordic writers. His father was a cobbler in the little port of Odense in the Great Belt, a wretchedly poor man who read a great deal and died when Hans was still a child. His mother remarried, became even more poverty stricken and took to drink.

Young Andersen was sent to a pauper school to become a tailor, but after a fortuneteller announced that Odense would one day hold him in great honor, he was allowed to go to Copenhagen. He tried acting, singing and finally playwriting but, unable even to spell, he proved a failure. When he was 17, an influential government minister, Jonas Collin, who had taken an interest in the boy, sent him to a grammar school, the Danish equivalent of a public academic high school. There he was so badly treated by the headmaster that he was removed to another school, and when he finally finished with school at the age of 23, he began writing again, mostly plays.

Andersen traveled widely, became a friend of Charles Dickens, fell in love with Jenny Lind, the Swedish opera singer, and was a frequent house guest in the country mansions of Denmark. He wrote a number of novels and poems, the best known of which is the Danish patriotic song *In Denmark I Was Born*. He told his mother's story in a tender and understated portrait called *She Was Worth Nothing*. His international reputation, however, rests on his short stories and fairy tales. In all he wrote 168 of these. Some were culled from the folk stories he had heard in his youth, but most were the product of his own vivid imagination, and although they often conceal a bitter comment on his own experiences or on contemporary events, they were all written in a style that was immediately intelligible to children. Like most great children's stories, many of them were told first and written down afterward, so that they have a direct and very simple style. Andersen was, in fact, a genius of simplicity, his early background never forgotten, never wholly discarded.

SØREN KIERKEGAARD, Andersen's contemporary, was a prolific writer on an entirely different plane. He rebelled against organized religion but remained a Christian while developing a philosophy emphasizing the importance of the individual and individual decision. His work was not well known in Europe for some years after his death because his many books were not translated even into German until the end of the 19th Century, but he laid the base for 20th Century Existentialism.

For three small countries to create so much of international standing in literature and thought, and all within the space of little more than half a century, is remarkable. But the period was one of great political and social change in Scandinavia, and it is often in such progressive periods that countries give birth to literary genius. A more stable area today, contemporary Scandinavia has not nurtured so many figures of such dimensions.

Among the few Scandinavian writers of truly international reputation in recent years have been Sigrid Undset of Norway and Pär Lagerkvist of Sweden. Miss Undset, who died in 1949, composed a series of historical and modern novels (*Kristin Lavransdatter*, *The Burning Bush*) deeply concerned with religion and ethical problems. Lagerkvist is a novelist, playwright, poet and critic who writes in a spare style of the eternal questions of good and evil and the nature of God and man.

Among Sweden's other contemporary writers are Gunnar Ekelöf, whose enigmatic poetry and lucid essays enjoy an ever-widening influence, and the poets Erik Lindegren and Harry Martinson. Denmark in the 20th Century produced the lyric poet Johannes V. Jensen; the dramatist Kaj Munk, a clergyman who was murdered by the Nazis in 1944; the storyteller Karen Blixen-Finecke, who wrote *Out of Africa* and *Seven Gothic Tales* under the name of Isak Dinesen; and the novelist Martin A. Hansen, who praised the life of the Middle Ages in contrast to contemporary civilization.

YEARNING FOR THE HOMELAND

A deep love for his Swedish home is expressed in Strindberg's play *Gustav Adolf* by the 17th Century king's chancellor while soldiering in Germany:

Is it too limited . . . our large country, whose borders and extent no one yet knows, where there is one man per square mile who longs for neighbors? Our forefathers, the Goths and the Northmen, emigrated because they found it too limited, but they were soon crushed by the streams of emigrants, were swallowed up, and didn't leave a trace after them. No, our land is big enough for the one who has a mind and spirit great enough to fill the empty expanses, and with great thoughts to populate the empty wilderness.

For me this rich land [Germany] with its white meat and its yellow wine is repulsive. I long for my native land with its black bread and its brown ale, and I shall thank God the day he lets me see again . . . Lake Mälar, with its great silence and its deep solitude.

The versatile H. C. Branner, a novelist, short-story writer and dramatist, is the best known of the living Danish writers. Major contemporary figures in Norway are the poet and novelist Tarjei Vesaas and Arnulf Øverland, unofficial poet laureate, who spent four years in a German concentration camp for his anti-Nazi activities.

Since most educated Scandinavians are fluent in English, there has been in recent years a large sale of American and British books, both clothbound and paperback. Not only are they sold in all three countries in their original editions, but the demand for reading material is so great and the local supply of talent so comparatively limited that translations of English and American books make up a large part of publishers' lists.

The theater also suffers from the relatively small size of its potential audience, and only Copenhagen measures up to what one expects of a capital city. With a quarter of Denmark's population concentrated there, the city is able to support six or seven commercial theaters, but it is the ballet rather than the legitimate stage that has caught the limelight. The Royal Danish Ballet, which in its present form was created in 1829 under the direction of August Bournonville (who choreographed no fewer than 53 ballets for it), has recently been influenced by Russian ballet. Nevertheless, it has developed a romantic style that, together with its dancers, is much appreciated in the other capitals of the world.

In Sweden, opera holds much the same position as the ballet holds in Denmark. The little

Drottningholm Theater just outside Stockholm, built in 1766 by Queen Lovisa Ulrika, is the best preserved court theater in the world, and the only one still functioning, complete with its original wooden stage machinery and its store of 30 stage sets dating from the 18th Century. The charm of its performances—mainly *opéra bouffe*—is enhanced by the fact that the attendants are dressed in reproductions of 18th Century costumes; another unusual feature is the depth of the stage, which almost equals that of the auditorium.

A few years after the Drottningholm Theater was built, Sweden's King Gustavus III founded the Royal Academy of Music. Attached to the academy, the Royal College of Music is the oldest of its kind outside of Italy. In 1773, Gustavus founded the Royal Opera. It was a great period for music in Sweden, setting the pattern for the present day; there are now about 100 municipal schools of music, and the Museum of Musical History in Stockholm has a superb selection of instruments which are periodically used in concerts.

JENNY LIND of Sweden, whose range and sweetness of tone made her the most renowned soprano of the late 19th Century, was the natural product of her country's musical enthusiasm. But the Norwegian soprano Kirsten Flagstad received her musical education abroad; although Norway produced the great lyrical composer Edvard Grieg and the violinist Ole Bull, it is the theater that receives most Norwegian public support. Government and municipal grants go to no fewer than seven theaters scattered up and down the country—in Trondheim, Bergen and Stavanger as well as Oslo. In 1948 Norway's Labor government established a traveling theater to tour the smaller towns, and in 1953 the same government founded a state theatrical school. Not until 1959 was there a permanent opera in Oslo. This began its life with Kirsten Flagstad as manager and producer.

In films Sweden, as might be expected of a more highly industrialized country, is preeminent; the Danes, however, were quicker to attempt the new medium. Their first film, on the life of the royal family, was made in 1898. Somewhat typically, Norway's first film, made in 1908, was called *Fiskerlivets Farer (The Dangers of a Fisherman's Life)*. Sweden's contribution to the art of the cinema is quite out of proportion to the country's size, and although its two greatest actresses—Greta Garbo and Ingrid Bergman—have stolen the popular limelight through their triumphs elsewhere, it is the Swedish directors who have given such distinction to the products of Sweden's own studios.

IN the silent era, there were Mauritz Stiller, who discovered Garbo, and Victor Sjöström, both men who helped to lift a mechanical contrivance to the level of art. Now Ingmar Bergman holds the torch; if he is not the greatest, certainly he is one of the greatest directors in the world today. Of his recent films, in which reality and fantasy are interwoven by poetic use of word and image, the most significant are *The Seventh Seal*, *Wild Strawberries*, *The Virgin Spring* and *The Silence*.

Of equal stature in Scandinavia on the documentary side—in prestige at any rate—is Arne Sucksdorff, who dazzled the world of international films with the beautiful simplicity of *The Great Adventure*, showing man's relationship to nature as children see it on a small farm. He capped that with *A Jungle Tale*, a story of life in a village in India. The Swedish studios produce about 20 films a year, and the quality of their directors is such that the standards maintained are well above the average of most countries.

The fields in which all three Scandinavian countries excel are architecture and design. This is an inherited instinct rather than an acquired art, having its root in the nature of the land and its raw materials of rock and wood, an instinct that led the Vikings to carve the beaks of their ships with strange devices and to decorate their sleds with intricate and beautiful designs. Scandinavians excelled in craftsmanship, fashioning functional things with the simplicity that is the hallmark of true beauty. Such objects as the lure, an artfully curved Danish musical instrument from the Bronze Age, the bronze-and-gold-ornamented Trundholm sun chariot from the same period and elaborately decorated gold horns dating from the Fifth Century A.D. all reflect their early mastery of design.

Working in stone and bronze and wood, the Nordic people maintained a high level of craftsmanship: the wood-and-elkhorn statue of St. George and the Dragon by Bernt Notke, erected in 1489 in the Great Church in Stockholm's ancient quarter, is probably the finest example of this sort of work in the world. They were skilled in architecture, too, as can be demonstrated by the beauty of the Norwegian stave churches and the older Danish churches, some almost Moorish in appearance, others built like fortresses, such as the unique round churches of the 12th Century, four of which remain well preserved on the island of Bornholm.

In the period after World War II, Denmark built up an international reputation in design, particularly for the clean, graceful lines of its furniture, whose style matched that of its functional buildings. Its architects were employed by many of the new countries—in Tunisia, for instance, the modern tourist hotels are Danish-designed and Danish-furnished—and this led to the growth of a large export industry.

MORE recently Sweden has excelled in industrial design. Very modern and very functional, with a simplicity that matches the materials now in general use, Swedish design is probably second only to Italian. The Swedes are proud of the community centers of Vällingby and Farsta, just outside Stockholm, which embody similar design skills.

In housebuilding the Swedes have developed the prefab (although not always with success) and even the build-it-yourself home. Like the Danes, they have used concrete and glass with striking ingenuity, even in their new churches, and have softened the effect with the generous use of wood.

In architectural style, the Norwegians are more stolid. Their industrial designs are also more conservative—possibly a reflection of Germanic influence from past centuries. The Oslo city hall, for instance, a square block built of intricately patterned brickwork with two squat towers, looks about as imposing as a warehouse coming in from the sea. And yet, characteristically, it is full of exciting murals depicting the life and history of the country, and the sculptures and fountains outside are arresting.

MORE than any other Scandinavians, the Norwegians have an affinity for the visual form of art, and nowhere else in the world is there a park like the Frogner in Oslo, an area of 74 acres laid out by Gustav Vigeland, Norway's greatest sculptor, and occupied by the bulk of his work. Altogether, there are 150 groups of massive, intertwined human figures. Vigeland's work may not be to everyone's taste, but the effect is impressive, even startling. Throughout the country, there is a passionate interest in sculpture and painting. Every town supports its own artists, and the houses of even average-income families contain original paintings. But with the notable exception of the works of the late Edvard Munch, a forerunner of German expressionism whose tortured work dealt with raw human emotions, the subjects tend to be sea- or mountainscapes, which is perhaps inevitable in view of the way the sea and the mountains dominate the whole of Norwegian life.

In general, the Norwegians are artistically perhaps the most individualistic of the Scandinavians. The Danes are certainly the most adaptable, the most open to outside influences. In recent years Sweden has not perhaps produced as much in the field of literature as it once did. It has been conjectured that the Swedes' creative abilities have been hampered by the fact that they did not participate in either World War I or World War II. In the fields of architecture and design, however, this is not true. Scandinavia as a whole seems to have drawn from its background of sea and forest a design form that is clear in line and strong in shape. This in the 20th Century may well prove to be its most important artistic contribution to the world.

Known by her pen name—Isak Dinesen—frail Danish Baroness Karen Blixen-Finecke wrote carefully textured baroque tales.

Creative Outburst in the Stolid North

Scandinavian art is not rich in masters or masterpieces, but the world would be very different had not Scandinavian artists pushed ahead in several important areas. Modern drama, for example, is almost unthinkable without Ibsen and Strindberg. Kierkegaard has deeply influenced 20th Century philosophy. Scandinavian design in furniture and home decoration has helped form modern taste. And these arts have shared a single purpose: to bring clarity and order into man's affairs, from the interior of his house to the most remote recesses of his mind and soul.

Bjørnstjerne Bjørnson, Norway's great 19th Century man of letters, sits in his study. Besides verse he turned out plays and novels.

MASTER PLAYWRIGHT, Henrik Ibsen wrote probing psychological studies of the individual's relation to society. They have profoundly influenced modern drama.

FURIOUS MISOGYNIST, August Strindberg of Sweden is still the subject of controversy for his dramas of the 1880s which savagely attack both women and marriage.

SUPERB STORYTELLER, Selma Lagerlöf is best known for *The Story of Gösta Berling* (1894), a historical novel based on legends and folk tales of her native Värmland.

FORCEFUL NOVELIST, Sigrid Undset of Norway, who died in 1949, is particularly renowned for her strong and factually accurate fiction dealing with medieval times.

Sweden's Pär Lagerkvist is perhaps Scandinavia's best and most noted living author. He has written plays, poems, stories and novels.

SWEDISH FILM MAKERS have brought a new seriousness to a challenging art

DIRECTOR Ingmar Bergman *(opposite)* thinks over a script change for his 1960 movie *The Devil's Eye*. He has written and directed more than 20 motion pictures.

ACTRESS Ingrid Thulin, although she has worked in Hollywood, made her reputation acting in Bergman's films and playing varied parts on the Stockholm stage.

DESIGNERS of homes, offices and useful household objects combine daring conception with meticulous craftsmanship

ARCHITECT Anders Tengbom *(opposite)* stands before the dramatic office building he designed for a Stockholm newspaper. Tengbom's father was also a leading architect and the two did a number of buildings together.

PRODIGY Arne Jacobsen of Denmark *(above)*, sitting in his famous "egg" chair, will attack any design problem. He has done textiles and lighting fixtures and built housing developments, private houses and town halls.

CABINETMAKER Hans Wegner from Denmark designs furniture with such simplicity and distinction that it approaches fine sculpture. One of his chairs has become a "classic" of modern design and is copied frequently.

YOUNG CERAMIST Gunilla Palmstierna *(above)*, already successful in her early thirties, produces vivid pottery in a studio in the artists' colony in Stockholm.

VERSATILE ARTIST Bjørn Wiinblad lays out mosaic tiles in the garden of his Copenhagen studio. He also paints, creates theater sets, and designs ceramics and textiles.

BRIGHT NEOPHYTE of Stockholm's textile designers, Hjördis Hjalmarsdotter *(opposite)* frequently turns her boldly colored fabrics into smart and unusual dresses.

BRILLIANT GLASSMEN survey their delicate and fanciful work *(above)* at the Orrefors company, the most famous of Sweden's noted glass-blowing establishments.

PER KROHG stands before a gay circus scene in this photograph made a few years before his death in 1965. Krohg was influenced by French painters, especially Matisse, but he was a Norwegian artist first and last, and painted many landscapes of his own country. His murals adorn buildings in Oslo and the U.N. headquarters in New York.

EDVARD MUNCH, who died in 1944, reveals his own tormented visionary mind in such nightmarish early canvases as *Jealousy (below)*, in which a man's head seems to be suspended between a flame-haired temptress and a powerful, bearded figure of evil authority. Munch's later work, like the painting above, was often less tortured.

10

A Future
Tied to
Trade

THE political and economic problems facing Scandinavia during the mid-1960s were formidable; more difficult probably than any that have arisen in the period since World War II. They mainly concerned the applications of Norway and Denmark for full membership in the Common Market and Sweden's request for a form of association that would preserve its neutrality. The fact that the negotiations were protracted caused much heart-searching and considerable political and financial rethinking in all three countries. And since the negotiations involved a grouping of the European nations with political union as a possible ultimate goal, they provided a fascinating insight into some of the problems and dilemmas that face Scandinavia today.

Since the war the three countries have devoted much energy to the development of co-operation among themselves, and in this more limited province of international relations they have had considerable success. In addition, all three countries have attained remarkable political stability at home. That this stability, together with good labor relations, has been bought at the price of higher production costs that will make it more difficult to maintain the competitive position of their exports is not the point. Internal stability exists, and it is on this basis—aided by the fact that all three countries have governments strongly oriented toward social welfare and are thus thinking politically along similar lines—that the recent close cooperation has developed.

The Nordic bloc, which includes Iceland and Finland, is very much a reality; it exists despite differences in its members' foreign and defense policies. The cooperation between the various countries rests on the Nordic Council which, since March 1962, has been broadened and strengthened by the Helsinki Treaty of Nordic Cooperation. Most important of all, the three countries have one fundamental policy in common. Because they all depend on exports to pay for essential raw materials and manufactured goods, they all believe passionately in a general policy of free trade.

THE importance of trade has been clear to the Nordic countries for centuries. In the early postwar years its significance was brought home to the people of Denmark and Norway by the Marshall Plan. The European Recovery Program, as it was officially called, was initiated in 1947, and for these two countries, exhausted by German occupation, it was a life line. Denmark invested nearly half its Marshall aid funds in purchases of fertilizers, fodder and agricultural equipment for its farmers. For Norway the plan meant food for its people and a start on reconstruction. Moreover, with Europe now in funds again, Norway benefited from the revitalization of trade throughout the western world, its ocean-going fleet being one of its chief economic assets.

The scale of Marshall aid was considerable, but even the $459 million received by Norway was only 10 per cent of that country's war losses. Nevertheless, it did give hope to an exhausted people and the real prospect at last of fighting their way back to some degree of prosperity and comfort. Both the Norwegians and Danes accepted the aid with gratitude.

Sweden, on the other hand, did not need direct Marshall aid, but it did need help of a different sort. It had come out of the war relatively unscathed and with its industries intact, but the German collapse and the poverty of its other traditional trading partners in Europe had undermined its foreign trade position. In 1945 it had granted credits to Denmark, Norway, Finland, France, the Netherlands and Great Britain, and by 1947 this had produced a foreign-exchange crisis in Stockholm. Sweden thereupon asked for and received a special Marshall Plan loan of $20.4 million to enable it to buy equipment from the United States. The loan, not due for final repayment until 1983, was completely paid up by the middle of 1962.

The Marshall Plan did more, however, than provide Europe with the funds its devastated and exhausted industries so desperately needed. It provided a stimulus for the more far-seeing to embark on the task of removing trade barriers and to take the first hesitant steps toward some form of political union. The plan was the dawn of a period of great opportunity that began with the formation of the European Coal and Steel Community in 1951 and progressed to the Treaty of Rome.

THIS treaty, signed in 1957 by the Benelux group—Belgium, the Netherlands and Luxembourg—with France, Italy and Western Germany, established what came to be known as the Common Market, or "the Inner Six." It could have been the first move in a union of almost all Europe, but the Inner Six were ready to work toward a much more binding economic unit than were the other European states. Britain and Scandinavia, in particular, were concerned about the possible political implications of the treaty, the preamble to which states that the signatories were "determined to establish the foundation of an ever closer union among the European peoples." In any event, they decided against membership at that stage.

The fact was that few politicians in these countries really believed the Common Market would ever come into existence in the first place, and when it did, few thought it would work. This was a fundamental error in political thinking, and when in the following year the Inner Six began the process of tearing down their intercommunity trade barriers and coordinating their tariffs against other countries, the remaining European nations were forced to recognize the economic danger of being outside such a close-knit and industrially powerful grouping. Under the leadership of Britain, the three Scandinavian countries, along with Austria, Switzerland and Portugal, formed the European Free Trade Association (Finland joined as an associate member in 1961), the purpose of which was to eliminate tariffs on industrial products among the member nations. EFTA, which became known as "the Outer Seven," was largely planned as a bargaining counter for later negotiations should the Common Market succeed in holding together.

It was obvious that EFTA was by no means as potent an economic grouping as the Six. The strength of the Common Market was that the Six constituted a centralized community of countries with common land frontiers and with harmonized economic policies. The Outer Seven, not integrated economically, were on the periphery of the Common Market, with only Britain and Scandinavia strategically grouped together. Also, they included three countries whose foreign policies were neutral and, therefore, at variance with those of the other EFTA members. For these neutral countries—Sweden, Austria and Switzerland—the success of the Common Market and the announcement in 1961 that Britain was applying to the Inner Six for membership raised special problems.

IN the field of international politics, Swedish neutrality is quite acceptable to the NATO powers, and apparently also to Russia since for them it secures the buffer position of Finland. Neutral as they are, the Swedes have the means, and one feels the will also, to fight if they are attacked. Swedish policy is directed toward two things: making the cost of invasion prohibitively expensive to any would-be aggressor and buying time until help comes if war occurs.

Nevertheless, most Swedes believe strongly in neutrality. Their prime minister, Tage Erlander, put their position firmly: "There can be no compromises over our traditional policy of neutrality." To be sure, their brand of neutrality is a special one. As a government spokesman remarked, "It goes without saying that Swedish neutrality is not characterized by any ideological 'neutralism.' Democratic Western ideals are living realities to the Swedish people, and we do not allow our attitude in foreign affairs to be determined by anxiety to find a compromise between democracy and dictatorship."

BECAUSE of their neutral stand, the Swedes were unable to follow Denmark and Norway when those countries, with Britain, applied for full membership in the Common Market. Instead, they applied for a form of associate membership, intent on protecting commercial relations with their two main trading partners, Britain and Germany, while still preserving their political neutrality. What made the situation particularly difficult were the conditions which Sweden placed on its prospective membership. First, it wanted to be able to make outside commercial agreements with nonmember countries, for example with members of the Soviet bloc, from which, among other things, it already buys oil. Second, it wanted to be able to quit the Common Market in case of war or similar crisis. Third, it wanted to be free to refrain from taking part in any economic measures dictated by political considerations—sanctions or boycotts, for example.

These were conditions which the Six were unlikely to accept in full, and this presented the Swedish government with a difficult choice. Exclusion from the Common Market would not only depress the country's economy but would appreciably limit its future growth. But membership, even on an associate basis, may be dependent on its giving up many of the rights it so far has considered essential. There are those, too, who feel that the pressures on Sweden for joining as a full-fledged member will ultimately prove irresistible and that the resulting abandonment of economic neutrality will inevitably result in a watering-down of Sweden's sacrosanct political neutrality.

Norway and Denmark, though they followed Britain's lead, approached the Common Market negotiations with their own share of soul-searching. Norwegians debated the move with surprising ferocity; their own independence from Sweden dates only from the beginning of this century and they were loath to see it curtailed in any way. But their overwhelming dependence on foreign trade finally carried the day. The Danes worried because exports mean everything to them, and Britain has long been the principal buyer of Danish agricultural products. But Denmark's European neighbors are also big purchasers. Thus when, in 1963, French President Charles de Gaulle vetoed Britain's application for membership in the Market, Denmark was faced with a very difficult decision: whether to join the Six by itself or to remain out in the cold with Britain.

LIKE Norway, Denmark chose to throw in its lot with the British. There were political as well as economic reasons for the choice. Government leaders felt that, in the Common Market as it stood, Germany, France and Italy were all weak on democracy; the politically stabilizing influence of Britain's membership was, therefore, essential to Denmark's entry. Scandinavia as a whole shared this sentiment.

Important changes were in the air of Western Europe. Economic cooperation had lost some of its political overtones, and there was a new "live and let live" attitude developing toward the East. While Russia in the 1940s and 1950s had loomed very large and menacingly in the minds of all Scandinavian politicians, the situation in the mid-1960s was much less threatening. East-West trade was on the increase. The Common Market appeared no longer as a political organization directed primarily against the Eastern countries, and talk about the "Iron Curtain" was not heard in everyday conversation as it once had been. In Denmark it was felt—and expressed by Prime Minister Jens Otto Krag—that NATO might look for aims other than defense and might even some day be able to mediate in the East-West dispute. Whether or not NATO as an organization was suitable for such a task remained questionable, but the mere fact that the idea could be brought up indicated the thaw.

As usual, trade was ahead of statesmanship. Scandinavian businessmen established contacts across borders, reaching as far as market agreements and bilateral treaties would allow. In Sweden this was cause for some unusual speculation about future relationships toward the rest of Europe. Clearly, Sweden's successful industrialists were anxious to see the country join the Six, although Swedish political leaders found it difficult to take the first step.

The key to further developments was Great Britain's admission to the Common Market, and to that end all of the Scandinavian countries looked hopefully for an improvement in French-British trade relations. Meanwhile, among the Northern states Sweden stood out as the one most interested in a Scandinavian Union, while Denmark and Norway remained understandably cool to the idea, fearing the wealth, power and ingenuity of the Swedes. However, all three countries appeared heading toward an increased measure of European cooperation in some form. The old aloofness is gone. "We cannot, simply because of progress already made, isolate ourselves from the rapid development of the rest of Europe," a Swedish trade union official said recently. "We do not want to become a sort of ethnographic museum piece visited by tourists wishing to see an idyllic political and social scene."

THE political and social idyll is after all dependent to a large extent on the maintenance of prosperity. And Scandinavia, however remote it may seem in the snow-clad mountains of the north, is still a part of Europe, and therefore affected by the permutations and combinations of European politics and economics. These, as always, remain fascinating and unpredictable.

A destroyer rests in one of Sweden's many bombproof docks. Next page: the liner "Kungsholm" leaves the harbor of Göteborg, Sweden.

SEAFARING NATIONS, *while protecting themselves in a time of peril . . .*

. . . also continue to expand their historic role as maritime powers, speeding their

own manufactures and the products of other nations across the world's oceans

Appendix

HISTORICAL DATES

A.D.

793-1066 Age of Viking raiding, trading and colonizing expeditions

c.800 Godfred rules as first Danish king

829 Ansgar, a Frankish monk, arrives in Sweden; his missionary activity represents a milestone in the gradual Christianization of Scandinavia

c.850-1000 Discovery of Iceland, Greenland and Vinland (North America)

872 King Harald Fairhair becomes first supreme ruler of Norway

935-985 Harald Bluetooth unites various kingdoms of Denmark

985-1014 Danish King Sven I defeats the Norwegians and Swedes and conquers England

1017-1035 Sven's son Canute the Great becomes king of Denmark, Norway and England. English artisans, architects, priests bring new influences to Scandinavia

1217-1263 Height of Norwegian royal power under King Haakon IV

1282 The Danish nobles force King Erik to recognize the national assembly and the subordination of the king to the law

1293 After more than a century of effort Sweden completes conquest of Finland

1332-1370 Economic and political rivalry between Denmark and north German towns of the Hanseatic League erupts into open war in which Denmark is the loser. League wins predominance in the Baltic

1349-1350 Bubonic plague, or "the Black Death," strikes Norway. The resulting depopulation of the farms, depriving the nobility of labor force and income, is a telling blow to feudalism

1350 Codification of Swedish national law helps unify the previously semiautonomous provinces

1397 Queen Margrethe establishes the Union of Kalmar, joining Denmark, Norway and Sweden under one crown

1477 The first university in Scandinavia is founded at Uppsala in Sweden

1520 After execution of Swedish nationalists in the "Massacre of Stockholm," Swedish peasants and miners, led by the nobleman Gustav Vasa, rebel against Danish rule

1523 Gustav Vasa elected king. Sweden secedes from Kalmar Union

1527 Lutheran Church is established in Sweden. Ten years later Denmark follows suit and forcibly introduces Lutheranism into Norway

1537 After a victorious war against Lübeck, leading city of the Hanseatic League, Gustavus I of Sweden ends the league's trade monopoly in the Baltic

1563-1660 Wars between Sweden and Denmark. At their end Denmark loses all of its northern provinces across the Sound which now separates the two nations

1611-1632 Sweden becomes the dominant power in the Baltic area under Gustavus II Adolphus, barring Russia from the Baltic Sea

1630 Sweden joins in Thirty Years' War, defending its Baltic empire and the Lutheran faith

1632 Gustavus II Adolphus, leading the victorious Swedes against the troops of the Holy Roman Emperor Ferdinand II, is killed in the Battle of Lützen

1638 First Swedish settlement in America founded on the Delaware River

1648 Treaty of Westphalia assigns part of northern Germany to Sweden

1697-1718 Charles XII of Sweden spends his reign fighting the "Great Nordic War" against Denmark-Norway, Poland-Saxony and Russia. After his death in battle, Sweden loses nearly all its overseas possessions and its great power position

1807 Bombardment of Copenhagen by English forces drives Denmark into alliance with Napoleon

1809 Sweden is forced to cede Finland after defeat in a 10-month war. The present Swedish constitution is adopted. It provides for separation between the king's executive power and that of parliament, and for an irremovable judiciary

1810 After a period of internal dissension over the succession to the Swedish throne, Jean Baptiste Bernadotte, one of Napoleon's marshals, is chosen heir. Eight years later he becomes king as Charles XIV John

1814 During the turmoils of the Napoleonic Wars Sweden wins control of Norway after a short struggle with Denmark. After

a brief Norwegian uprising, a compromise is reached under which the two countries are to be ruled by the Swedish royal house. Norway keeps its own constitution and parliament

1860s Crop failures and poverty of the landless Swedish farm workers set off an emigration wave which eventually takes 1.5 million Swedes to the U.S.

1864 Denmark loses the duchies of Schleswig and Holstein in a war with Prussia and Austria

1871 Danish Social-Democratic party founded

1887 Norwegian Labor party founded

1889 The Social-Democratic party is formed in Sweden. Within the decade the important Trade Union Federation and the Consumers' Cooperative Association are founded

1891-1892 Denmark passes old-age pension and health insurance laws

1905 Norway, to protect its expanding trade and seafaring interests, demands a consular service separate from Sweden's. Dispute with Sweden leads to Norway's independence. Prince Carl of Denmark is elected Norway's king as Haakon VII

1914-1918 The three Scandinavian monarchies maintain neutrality during World War I

1936 Old-age pensions and unemployment insurance are introduced in Norway

1939-1945 World War II. Denmark and Norway are attacked and occupied by Germany. Sweden manages to remain outside the conflict

1946 Sweden, Norway and Denmark join the United Nations

1949 Norway and Denmark, refusing to join Scandinavian neutral defense organization proposed by Sweden, become members of NATO. Sweden stays out

1952 Nordic Council for economic, social and cultural cooperation is ratified by Denmark, Norway, Sweden and Iceland. Finland becomes a member four years later

1961 Denmark and Norway apply for membership in the European Economic Community—the Common Market. Sweden applies for a form of associate membership

FOR FURTHER READING

CHAPTER 1: THE THREE KINGDOMS

American-Scandinavian Review, The. A quarterly published by The American-Scandinavian Foundation, New York.

De Maré, Eric, *Scandinavia.* Hastings, 1955.

Jensen, Amy E., *Iceland.* Exposition Press, 1954.

Mead, W. R., *An Economic Geography of the Scandinavian States and Finland.* University of London Press, 1964.

Mortensen, Sverre, ed., *The Norway Year Book.* Johan Grundt Tanum Forlag, Oslo, 1962.

Ogrizek, Doré, ed., *Scandinavia.* McGraw-Hill, 1952.

Rodnick, David, *The Norwegians.* Public Affairs Press, Washington, D.C., 1955.

Scandinavia Past and Present. E. H. Arnkrone, Odense, 1959.

Scandinavian States and Finland, The. Royal Institute of International Affairs, London and New York, 1951.

Wuorinen, John H., *Scandinavia.* Prentice-Hall, 1965.

CHAPTER 2: THE VIKING AGE

Arbman, Holger, *The Vikings.* Frederick A. Praeger, 1961.

Brøndsted, Johannes, *The Vikings.* Penguin Books, 1965.

Ingstad, Helge M., *Land Under the Pole Star.* St. Martin's Press, 1966.

Mowat, Farley, *Westviking.* Little, Brown, 1965.

Oxenstierna, Eric, *The Norsemen.* New York Graphic Society, 1965.

Pohl, Frederick J., *The Viking Explorers.* Thomas Y. Crowell, 1966.

CHAPTER 3: UNITY AND DISUNITY

Andersson, Ingvar, *A History of Sweden.* Frederick A. Praeger, 1956.

Arneson, Ben A., *The Democratic Monarchies of Scandinavia.* D. Van Nostrand, 1949.

Johnson, Amanda, *Norway, Her Invasion and Occupation.* Bowen Press, 1948.

Koht, Halvdan, and Sigmund Skard, *The Voice of Norway.* Columbia University Press, 1944.

Larsen, Karen, *A History of Norway.* The American-Scandinavian Foundation, New York, 1950.

Lauring, Palle, *A History of the Kingdom of Denmark.* Høst & Son, Copenhagen, 1960.

Shirer, William L., *The Challenge of Scandinavia.* Little, Brown, 1955.

CHAPTER 4: DENMARK

Danstrup, John, *History of Denmark.* Wivel, Copenhagen, 1948.

Denmark. Royal Danish Ministry of Foreign Affairs, Copenhagen, 1961.

Greenland. Royal Danish Ministry of Foreign Affairs, Copenhagen, 1961.

Halck, Niels, *Social Welfare in Denmark.* The Danish Ministries of Labor and Social Affairs, Copenhagen, 1961.

Industrial Denmark. Federation of Danish Industries, Copenhagen, 1961.

CHAPTER 5: NORWAY

Collinder, Björn, *The Lapps.* Princeton University Press for The American-Scandinavian Foundation, 1949.

Derry, T. K., *A Short History of Norway.* Hillary House, 1960.

Dorfman, Herbert, *Labor Relations in Norway.* The Norwegian Joint Committee on International Social Policy, Oslo, 1958.

Grimley, O. B., *Co-operatives in Norway.* The Co-operative Union and Wholesale Society, Oslo, 1950.

Norwegian System of Social Insurance, The. The National Insurance Institution, Oslo, 1961.

Vogt, Per, ed., *Norway Today.* Dreyer, Oslo, 1961.

CHAPTER 6: SWEDEN

Andersson, Ingvar, *Introduction to Sweden.* Bedminster Press, 1962.

Heckscher, E. F., *An Economic History of Sweden.* Harvard University Press, 1954.

Johnston, T. L., *Collective Bargaining in Sweden.* Harvard University Press, 1962.

Kastrup, Allan, *Digest of Sweden.* The American-Swedish News Exchange, New York, 1965.

Nelson, George R., ed., *Freedom and Welfare, Social Patterns in the Northern Countries of Europe.* The Northern Ministries of Social Affairs, Copenhagen, 1953.

Oakley, Stewart, *A Short History of Sweden.* Frederick A. Praeger, 1966.

Social Benefits in Sweden. The Swedish Institute and Framtiden Life Insurance Company, Stockholm, 1966.

Strode, Hudson, *Sweden: Model for a World.* Harcourt, Brace, 1949.

CHAPTER 7: PERSONALITIES OF PEACE

Bergengren, Erik, *Alfred Nobel.* Thomas Nelson and Sons, 1962.

Halasz, Nicholas, *Nobel.* Orion Press, 1959.

Hewins, Ralph, *Count Folke Bernadotte.* T. S. Denison, Minneapolis, 1950.

Høyer, Liv Nansen, *Nansen, A Family Portrait by His Daughter.* Longmans, London, 1957.

Lash, Joseph P., *Dag Hammarskjöld.* Doubleday, 1961.

Lie, Trygve, *In the Cause of Peace.* Macmillan, 1954.

Partridge, Bellamy, *Amundsen.* Robert Hale, London, 1953.

CHAPTER 8: FORESTS AND WATER

Facts About Denmark. Politiken's Forlag, Copenhagen, 1962.

Facts About Sweden. The Swedish Institute, Stockholm, 1966.

Sanderson, Ivan T., *Follow the Whale.* Little, Brown, 1956.

Streyffert, Thorsten, *Forestry in Sweden.* Oregon State College School of Forestry, 1958.

Villiers, Alan, *Whaling in the Frozen South.* Bobbs-Merrill, Indianapolis, 1925.

Westerlind, Erik, and Rune Beckman, *Sweden's Economy: Structure and Trends.* Prisma and The Swedish Institute, Stockholm, 1965.

Wold, Ragnar, ed., *Facts About Norway.* Chr. Schibsteds Forlag, Oslo, 1960.

CHAPTER 9: CULTURAL HISTORY

Alander, Bo, *Swedish Music.* The Swedish Institute, Stockholm, 1956.

Beyer, Harald, *A History of Norwegian Literature.* New York University Press for The American-Scandinavian Foundation, 1956.

Contemporary Danish Prose. An anthology, Gyldendal, Copenhagen, 1958.

Gustafson, Alrik, *A History of Swedish Literature.* University of Minnesota Press, 1961.

Hård af Segerstad, Ulf, *Scandinavian Design.* Nordisk Rotogravyr, Stockholm, 1961.

Horton, John, *Scandinavian Music: A Short History.* Norton, 1964.

Hunter, Leslie S., ed., *Scandinavian Churches.* Augsburg, 1965.

Lange, Kristian, and Arne Østvedt, *Norwegian Music.* Dobson, London, 1958.

McFarlane, James Walter, *Ibsen and the Temper of Norwegian Literature.* Oxford University Press, 1960.

Mitchell, P. M., *A History of Danish Literature.* Gyldendal, Copenhagen, 1957.

Paulsson, Thomas, *Scandinavian Architecture.* Charles T. Branford, Newton, Mass., 1959.

Stenstadvold, Håkon, *Norwegian Paintings.* Dreyer, Oslo, 1951.

Wilson, David, and Ole Klindt-Jensen, *Viking Art.* Cornell University Press, 1966.

CHAPTER 10: SCANDINAVIA TODAY

Andrén, Nils, *Government and Politics in the Nordic Countries.* Almquist and Wiksell/Gebers, Stockholm, 1964.

Lindgren, Raymond E., *Norway-Sweden, Union, Disunion and Scandinavian Integration.* Princeton University Press, 1959.

Wendt, Frantz, *The Nordic Council and Co-operation in Scandinavia.* Munksgaard, Copenhagen, 1965.

FAMOUS SCANDINAVIAN CULTURAL FIGURES AND THEIR PRINCIPAL WORKS

MUSIC

Roman, Johan-Helmich	1694-1758	The "father of Swedish music," pupil of Handel, composer of sacred and secular music
Berwald, Franz	1796-1868	Sweden's greatest composer of the classic period. He wrote symphonies and chamber music
Gade, Niels V.	1817-1890	Danish composer of cantatas: *Elverskud, Spring Message*
Grieg, Edvard	1843-1907	Composer, strongly influenced by Norwegian folk tunes: *Peer Gynt* orchestral suites, *Norwegian Dances*, ballads
Sinding, Christian	1856-1941	Norwegian composer in a late-romantic style. Orchestral and piano music: *Rustle of Spring*
Rosenberg, Hilding	1892-	Composer of a modern Swedish choral symphony: *The Revelation of St. John*
Riisager, Knudåge	1897-	Danish composer. Ballet music: *Slaraffenland*. Concert overture: *Erasmus Montanus*

PAINTING AND SCULPTURE

Roslin, Alexander	1718-1793	Swedish portraitist of the French school: *Lady With Veil, Empress Catherine of Russia*
Sergel, Johan Tobias	1740-1814	Swedish neoclassic sculptor: statue of *King Gustaf III* in Stockholm harbor
Thorvaldsen, Bertel	1770-1844	Danish sculptor. He lived most of his life in Rome and became the foremost sculptor of his time: *The Three Graces, Night and Day*
Dahl, Johan Christian	1788-1857	Norwegian painter of grand and dramatic landscapes: *Mountains at Stalheim*
Sonne, Jørgen Valentin	1801-1890	Danish painter of rural scenes. Frieze: *Thorvaldsen's Return to Copenhagen*
Hill, Carl Fredrik	1849-1911	Swedish painter of silvery trees and sun-baked beaches. His work foreshadows later expressionism and surrealism
Krohg, Christian	1852-1925	Norwegian painter with robust, impressionistic style: *Albertine, Svart-Anna*
Munch, Edvard	1863-1944	Norway's foremost postimpressionist painter. His early work *Spring* and large canvases in the University of Oslo are among his best-known paintings
Vigeland, Gustav	1869-1943	The most vigorous personality in Norwegian sculpture of his day. His early delicate portrait sculptures were followed by heavy, massive figures for Oslo's Frogner Park
Milles, Carl	1875-1955	Swedish-born sculptor, creator of fountains for many Swedish and American towns
Krohg, Per	1889-1965	Norwegian painter, son of Christian Krohg: murals in Oslo's Town Hall and University

ARCHITECTURE AND DESIGN

Anonymous	c.1100	Norwegian stave churches. Highly original wood constructions often decorated with pagan animal ornaments. The churches at Urnes and Borgund are examples
Anonymous	13th Century	Cathedral at Uppsala, Sweden, in pure Gothic style
King Christian IV	1588-1648	One of Denmark's greatest builders. He drew the plans for the Rosenborg Palace, the Copenhagen Exchange, Copenhagen University and its Trinitatis Church
Tessin, Nikodemus, the Elder	1615-1681	Architect of Swedish manor houses and castles: Drottningholm Castle and Kalmar Cathedral
Tessin, Nikodemus, the Younger	1654-1728	Swedish architect: Stockholm's Royal Palace and Great Church
Hansen, C. F.	1765-1845	Danish neoclassic architect: Town Hall and Court House in Copenhagen
Jensen, Georg	1866-1935	Danish pioneer designer and master craftsman: silver
Östberg, Ragnar	1866-1945	Swedish architect: Stockholm's City Hall
Måås-Fjetterström, Märta	1873-1941	Swedish textile designer
Poulsson, Magnus	1881-1958	Norwegian architect. With Arnstein Arneberg he designed the Oslo City Hall. His shingled village church at Gravberget fits beautifully into the surrounding forest landscape
Hald, Edward	1883-	Glass designer. He first earned Sweden its name for fine glassware
Asplund, Gunnar	1885-1940	Swedish architect: Stockholm's city library, chapels at Forest Crematorium
Klint, Kaare	1888-1954	Danish architect and furniture designer. He greatly influenced modern furniture design
Kåge, Wilhelm	1889-1960	Swedish ceramist, largely responsible for the rebirth of Swedish ceramic production
Markelius, Sven	1889-	Swedish architect and city planner. He drew the plans for modernizing central Stockholm and for the self-contained Stockholm suburb, Vällingby
Lauritzen, Vilhelm	1894-	Architect of Copenhagen's Radio House and of the Danish embassy in Washington, D.C.
Krebs, Nathalie	1895-	Danish ceramist. A chemist and glaze specialist, she started the Saxbo workshop
Jacobsen, Arne	1902-	Danish architect: the Bellevue Strand Bath and theater. The Aarhus Town Hall designed by him and Erik Møller is considered one of the finest examples of modern Danish architecture
Juhl, Finn	1912-	Danish architect and furniture designer. He designed the interior of the Trusteeship Council chamber at the United Nations and the furniture for the Danish embassy in Washington, D.C.
Wegner, Hans	1914-	Danish architect, cabinetmaker and furniture designer: conference room at UNESCO headquarters in Paris
Lindberg, Stig	1916-	Versatile Swedish designer of ceramic ornaments, bone china, textiles, playing cards
Korsmo, Grete Prytz	1917-	Norwegian designer of silver and enamel bowls, vases and jewelry
Eckhoff, Tias	1926-	Norwegian designer of porcelain, ceramic, silver and teakwood objects

LITERATURE

Anonymous	900-1050	*Edda.* Norwegian-Icelandic myths about Norse Gods and legendary heroes, in poetic form
Sturluson, Snorri	1179-1241	Greatest of the Icelandic historians, whose chief works are *Heimskringla (Circle of the World)*, an epic history of the Norwegian kings, and prose *Edda*
Saxo Grammaticus	c.1200	*Gesta Danorum (The Deeds of the Danes)*, a history of Denmark from legendary times to the author's day

Holberg, Ludvig	1684-1754	Norwegian-born poet and professor. He wrote more than 30 comedies and is considered the founder of the Danish-Norwegian theater: *Jeppe of the Hill*
Swedenborg, Emanuel	1688-1772	Swedish scientist, mystic and religious philosopher: *De cultu et amore Dei*
Linné, Carl von (Linnaeus)	1707-1778	Originator of a botanical classification system and author of travel reports of literary interest
Bellman, Carl Michael	1740-1795	One of Sweden's greatest poets. Wrote gay and melancholy songs about tavern life in the pleasure-loving Stockholm of his day: *Fredman's Epistles, Fredman's Songs*
Tegnér, Esaias	1782-1846	Swedish romantic poet. He made a passionate patriotic appeal in his poem *Svea* and reflected on past greatness in *Fritiof's Saga*
Runeberg, Johan Ludvig	1804-1877	Epic patriotic poetry: *The Tales of Ensign Stål*
Andersen, Hans Christian	1805-1875	Denmark's most famous storyteller: *The Match Girl, The Emperor's Clothes*
Welhaven, Johan Sebastian	1807-1873	Danish-oriented Norwegian author of essays, criticism and lyrical poetry. Cycle of sonnets: *Norway's Dawn*, satirizing Norwegian provincialism
Wergeland, Henrik	1808-1845	Norwegian nationalist poet. Dramatic epics: *Creation, Man and Messiah*, followed by patriotic poems that became an inspiration during the Nazi occupation of Norway
Kierkegaard, Søren	1813-1855	Danish religious thinker, one of the precursors of existentialism: *The Concept of Dread, The Sickness Unto Death, Either-Or*
Ibsen, Henrik	1828-1906	Norwegian dramatist whose work marks the beginning of modern prose drama: *Pillars of Society, A Doll's House, Ghosts, An Enemy of the People, The Wild Duck, Hedda Gabler.* Verse dramas: *Brand, Peer Gynt*
Bjørnson, Bjørnstjerne	1832-1910	Poet, playwright, politician. Short stories and poems on national and romantic subjects. Dramas dealing with Norwegian social problems: *Beyond Our Power, The Bankrupt*
Lie, Jonas	1833-1908	Novels about northern Norway and social controversies: *The Family at Gilje*
Brandes, Georg	1842-1927	Danish literary critic with great influence on modern literature in Scandinavia: *Main Currents in Nineteenth Century European Literature*
Jacobsen, Jens Peter	1847-1885	Danish novelist: *Niels Lyhne, Marie Grubbe*
Strindberg, August	1849-1912	Playwright. Renewed Swedish prose style and poetry, influenced European drama. Biting social criticism expressed in the novel *The Red Room*. Prose polemic: *The New Kingdom.* Naturalistic dramas: *Miss Julie, The Father*. Expressionistic drama: *A Dream Play*
Garborg, Arne	1851-1925	Norwegian poet: "Haugtussa," about life in a rural community
Pontoppidan, Henrik	1857-1943	Danish neoclassicist: *Lykke-Per (Lucky Per)*
Lagerlöf, Selma	1858-1940	Inspired Swedish storyteller: *The Story of Gösta Berling, Jerusalem, The Wonderful Adventures of Nils*
Hamsun, Knut	1859-1952	Norwegian neoromanticist. Sensitively described nature in novels about the soil and the sea: *Hunger, Pan, The Growth of the Soil*
Fröding, Gustaf	1860-1911	Swedish poet. His rhythmic verse covers a wide range of subjects with humor and compassion: *Guitar and Concertina, New Poems*
Andersen Nexø, Martin	1869-1954	Danish social reformer. Novels: *Pelle the Conqueror, Ditte, Child of Man*
Duun, Olav	1876-1939	Novels about Norway's Namdal region: *The People of Juvik*, the saga of a family in a farming community
Undset, Sigrid	1882-1949	Novels of medieval Norway: *Kristin Lavransdatter, Olav Audunssøn*
Bergman, Hjalmar	1883-1931	Brilliantly comic novels with a fatalistic undertone: *God's Orchid, Thy Rod and Thy Staff.* Play: *Swedenhielms*
Blixen-Finecke, Karen (Isak Dinesen)	1885-1962	Danish storyteller: *Seven Gothic Tales, Winter Tales, Out of Africa*
Øverland, Arnulf	1889-	Norwegian author. His 1936 poem *You Must Not Sleep* warned against the rising powers of destruction in Europe
Lagerkvist, Pär	1891-	Swedish literary expressionist. Drama: *The Man Without a Soul.* Arresting modern prose parables about God, man and evil: *The Dwarf, Barabbas.* Poetry: *Evening Land*
Södergran, Edith	1892-1923	Poems in Swedish. This Finnish author opened the modern era in Swedish poetry: *The Land That Is Not*
Petersen, Nis	1897-1943	Danish historical novelist: *The Street of the Sandalmakers.* Lilting poetry: *Night Pipets*
Vesaas, Tarjei	1897-	Norwegian novelist: *The House in the Dark*, about the German occupation of Norway. Short stories: *Vindane (The Winds)*
Moberg, Vilhelm	1898-	Swedish novelist. He defends individualism against modern bureaucracy in epic novels about country people: *The Earth Is Ours, The Emigrants, The Last Letter to Sweden*
Munk, Kaj	1898-1944	Danish clergyman, journalist, dramatist. Historical drama: *Herod the King.* Modern miracle play: *The Word*
Grieg, Nordahl	1902-1943	Norwegian poet and playwright. His poems were an inspiration to Norwegians during the German occupation in World War II: *Norway in Our Hearts.* Play: *Defeat*
Martinson, Harry	1904-	Swedish author. Sensitive accounts of his orphaned childhood and years at sea: *Flowering Nettle, The Way Out.* Verse epic: *Aniara*, fantasy set in a space ship. Poetry: *Dreamers and Daddy Long-Legs*
Hansen, Martin A.	1905-1955	Danish author of novels and essays contrasting modern civilization with the integrated culture of the Middle Ages. Novels: *Jonathan's Journey, The Liar*
Ekelöf, Gunnar	1907-	Swedish poet with great influence on the younger generation of writers: *Late on Earth, Bu, The Blind Man's Song, Ferry Song*
Lidman, Sara	1923-	Swedish author of novels dealing with rural life in the province of Västerbotten: *The Tar Still, Cloudberry Land, The Rain Bird*

Credits

The sources for the illustrations in this book are shown below: Credits for pictures from left to right are separated by commas, top to bottom by dashes.

Cover—Howard Sochurek
8, 9—Louise Dahl-Wolfe
15—Marvin E. Newman
16—Brassai from Rapho Guillumette
17, 18, 19—Marvin E. Newman
20, 21—Ernst Haas from Magnum
22, 23—Howard Sochurek
24 through 27—Marvin E. Newman
28, 29—Culver Pictures
32—Map by Bill Dove
37—Marvin E. Newman
38, 39—Danish National Museum except top left; Statens Historiska Museum center; Erik Liljeroth
40—Larry Burrows
41—Marvin E. Newman
42—Mark Kauffman
45, 46—The Bettmann Archive
47, 48—Culver Pictures
52, 53, 54—Erik Liljeroth
55—Brassai from Rapho Guillumette
56—Chris Kendahl from Europress—James Whitmore
57—Marvin E. Newman
58, 59—Nina Leen except right, Marvin E. Newman
60—Marvin E. Newman
63—Culver Pictures
68—Henri Cartier-Bresson
69 through 72—Marvin E. Newman
73—James Whitmore
74, 75—Tore Johnson
78, 79—Illustration by Johan Turi from *Turi's Book of Lappland* Harper & Row
81—Marvin E. Newman
82, 83—Marvin E. Newman,

Howard Sochurek
84—David Moore from Black Star
85—Brian Seed
86—Carl Mydans
93 through 97—Marvin E. Newman
98, 99—John Sadovy
100—Larry Burrows
107—Copyright Philippe Halsman
108, 109—H. Aschehoug & Co. except bottom center; United Nations High Commissioner for Refugees, bottom right—United Press International
110—Larry Burrows except top left; Wide World Photos
111—Larry Burrows
112—Karl Gullers from Rapho Guillumette
119 through 125—Howard Sochurek
126—Marvin E. Newman
133—Pierre Boulat
134—The Bettmann Archive—United Press International, Brown Brothers
135—The Bettmann Archive, Louise Dahl-Wolfe—Lennart Nilsson
136—Lennart Nilsson
137 through 142—Marvin E. Newman
143—Courtesy Sonja Henie—Niels Onstad Collection—courtesy Minneapolis Institute of Arts, the Lillian Z. Turnblad Fund
144—Marvin E. Newman
149—Wide World Photos
150, 151—Marvin E. Newman

ACKNOWLEDGMENTS

The editors of this book are indebted to John Wuorinen, Professor of History, Columbia University, and to Leif T. I. Sjöberg, Assistant Professor of Swedish Language and Literature, Columbia University. Both read and commented on portions of the text.

xx

Production staff for Time Incorporated

John L. Hallenbeck (Vice President and Director of Production)

Robert E. Foy, Caroline Ferri and Robert E. Fraser

Text photocomposed under the direction of

Albert J. Dunn and Arthur J. Dunn